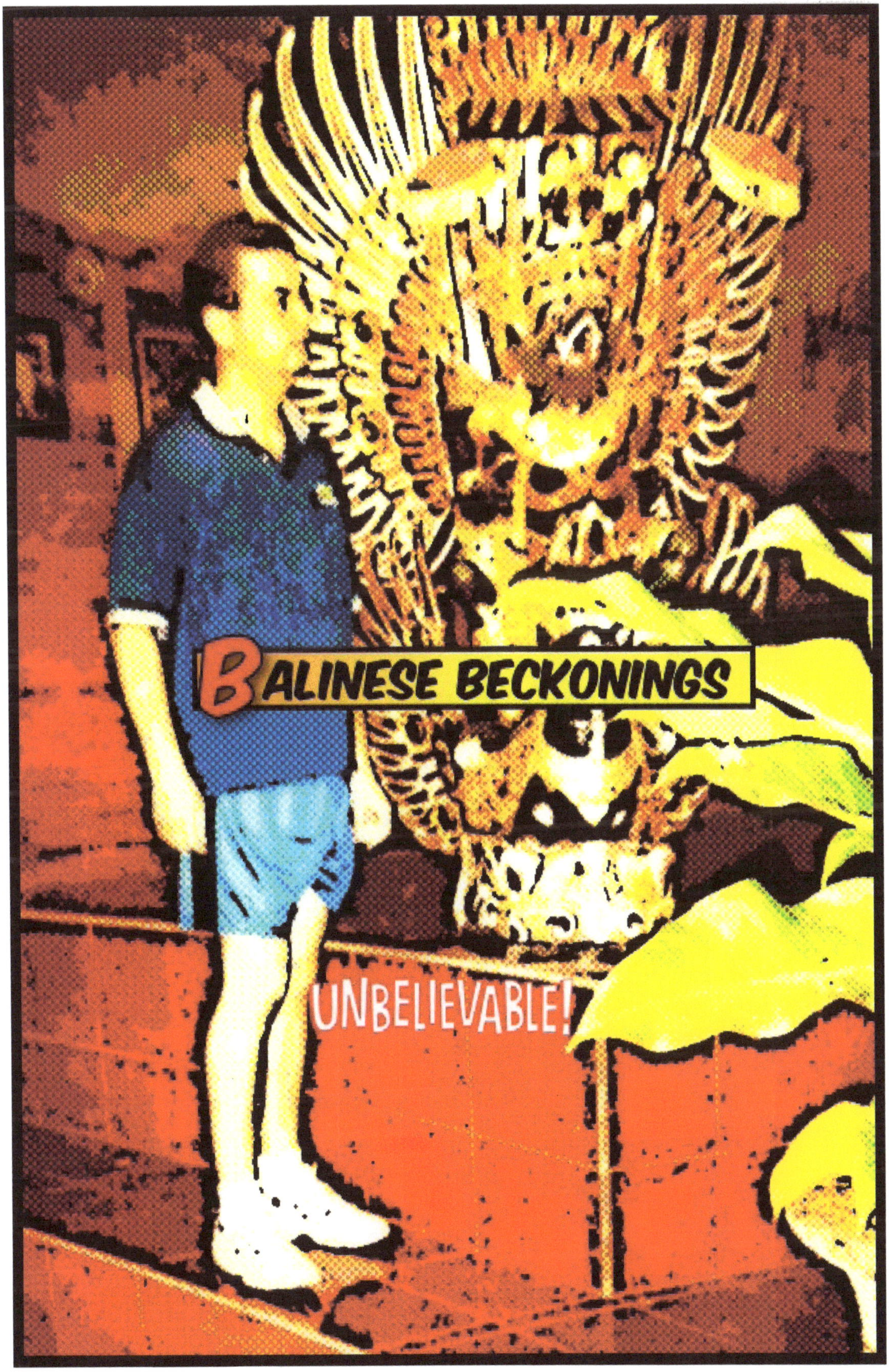
BALINESE BECKONINGS
UNBELIEVABLE!

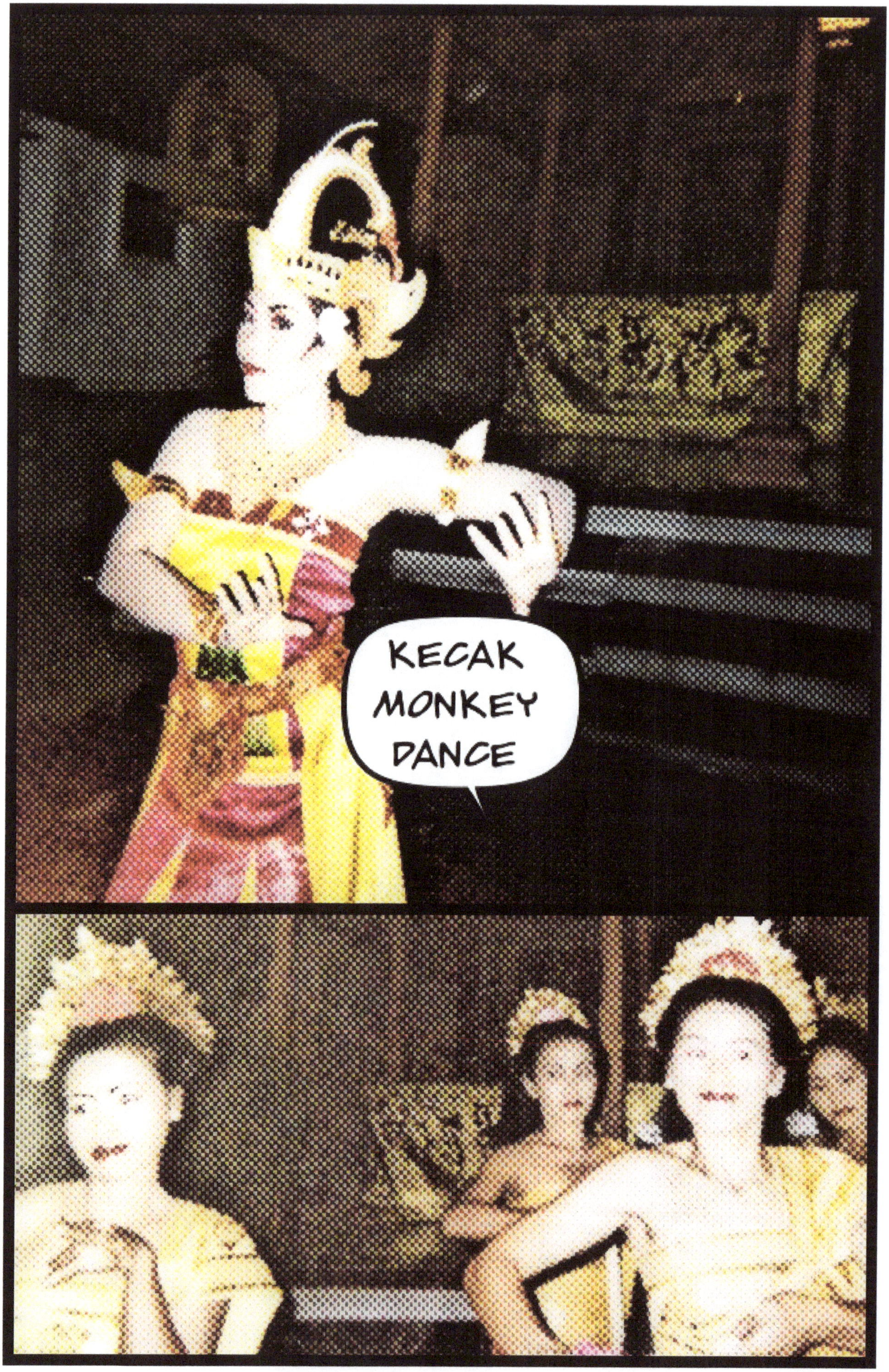
KECAK MONKEY DANCE

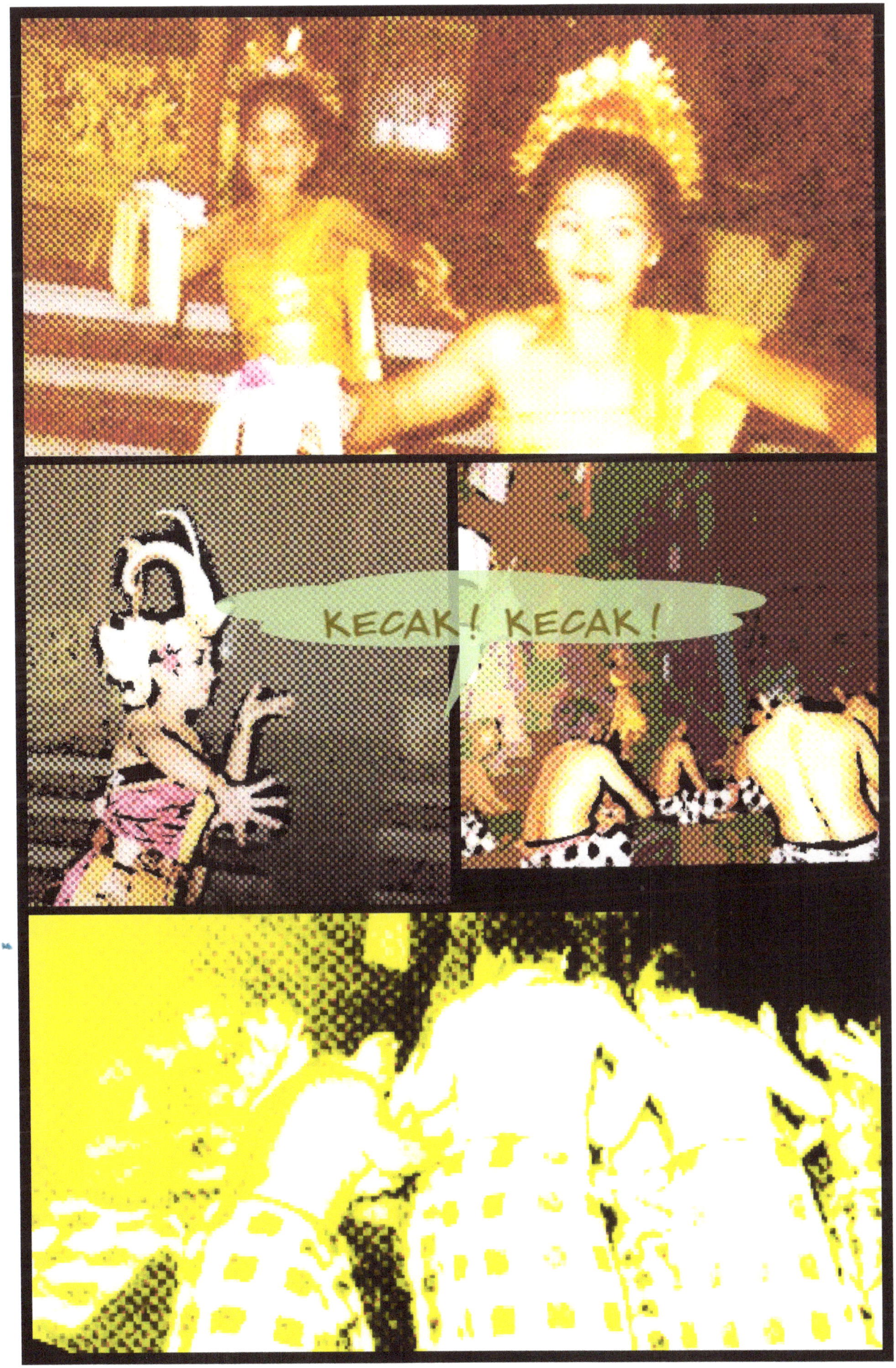
KECAK! KECAK!

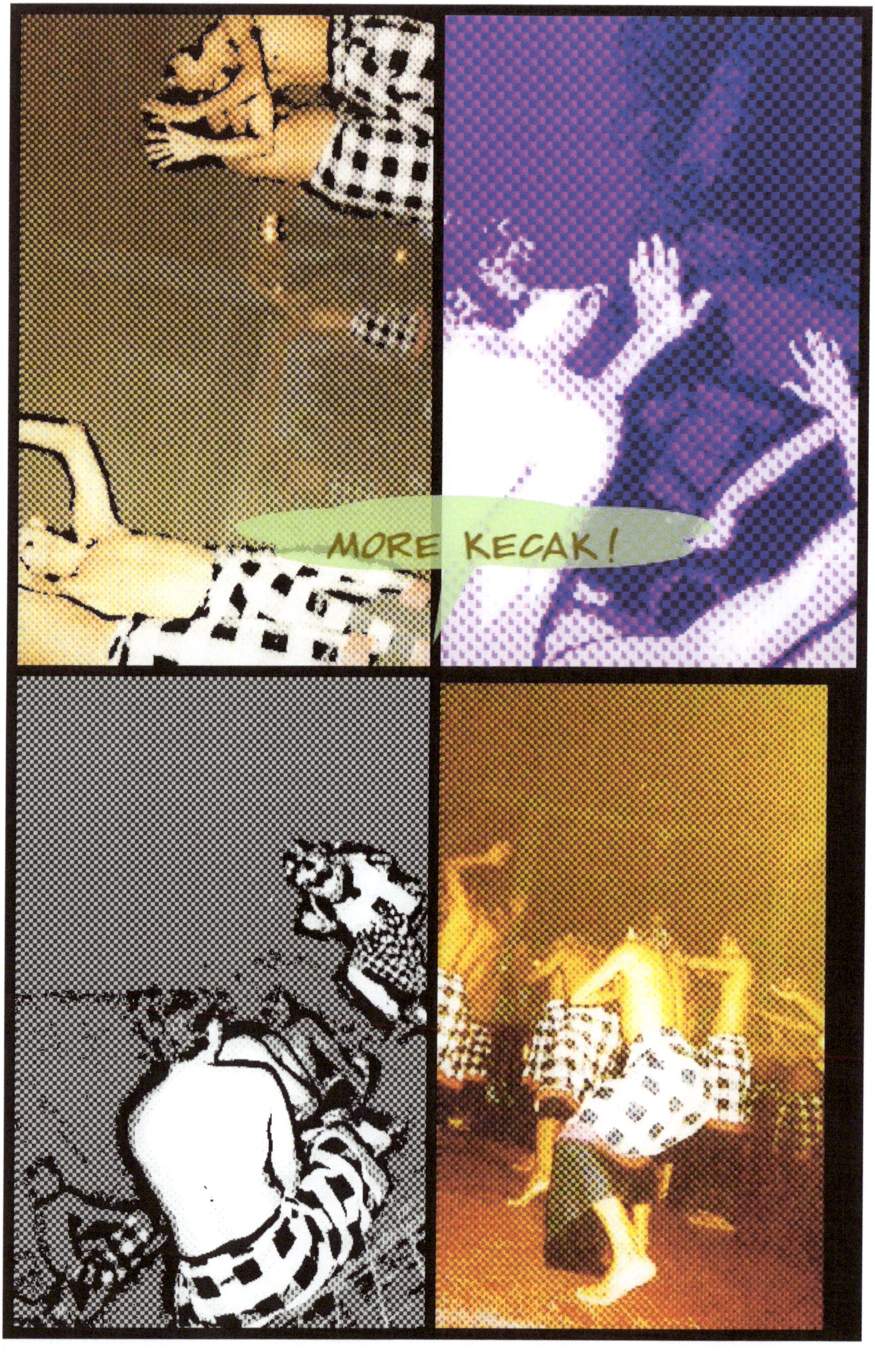
MORE KECAK!

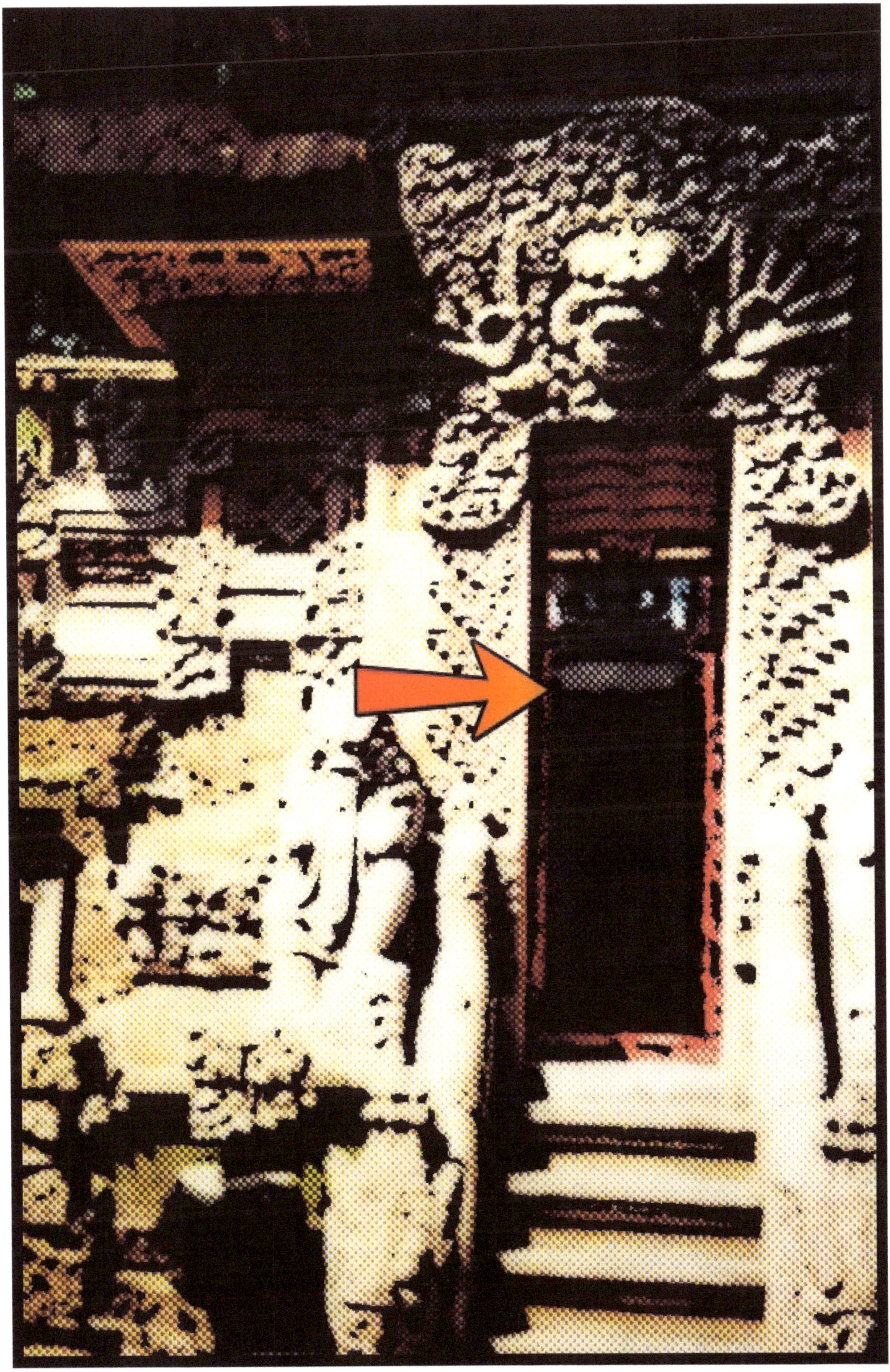

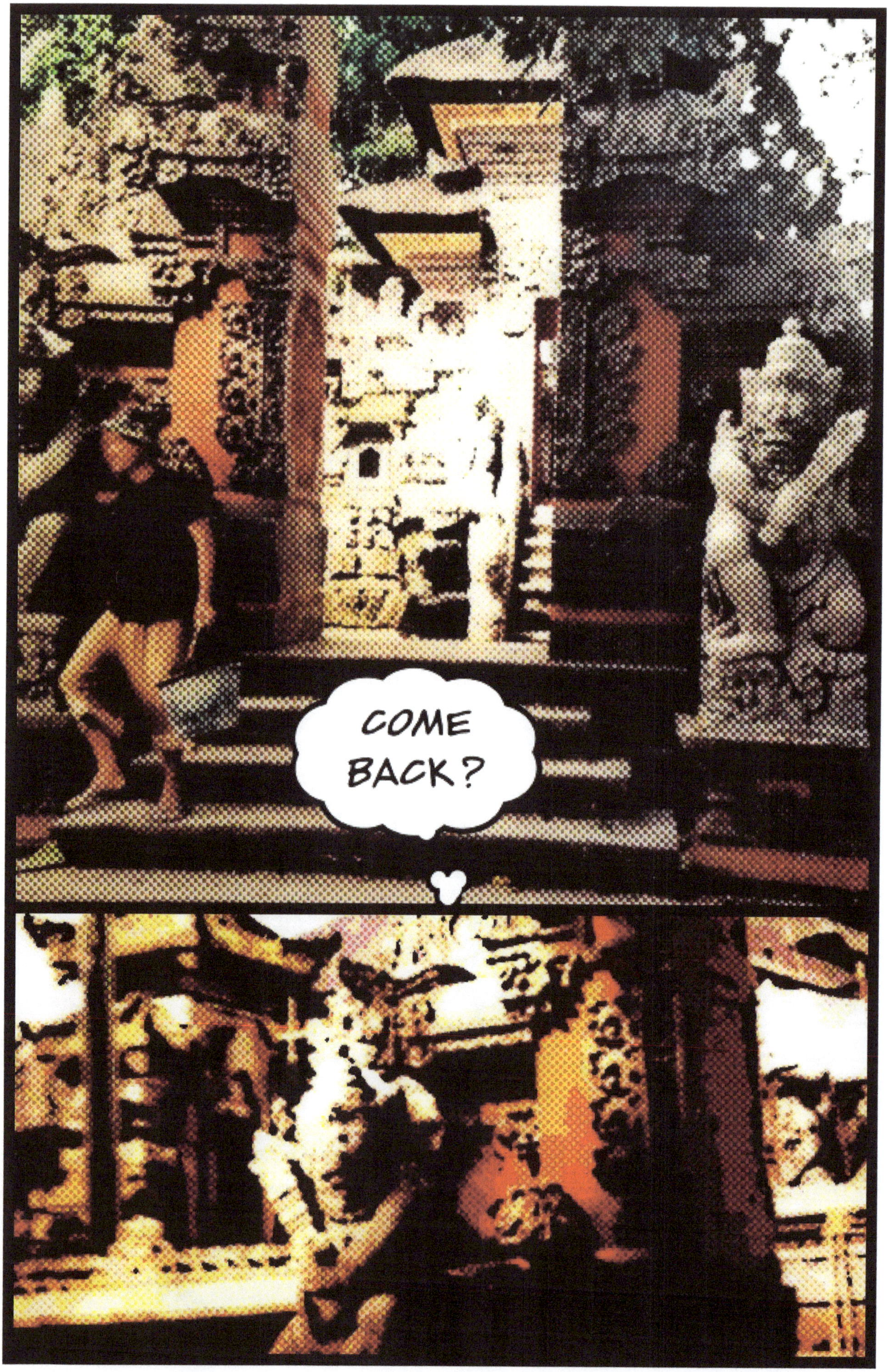
COME BACK?

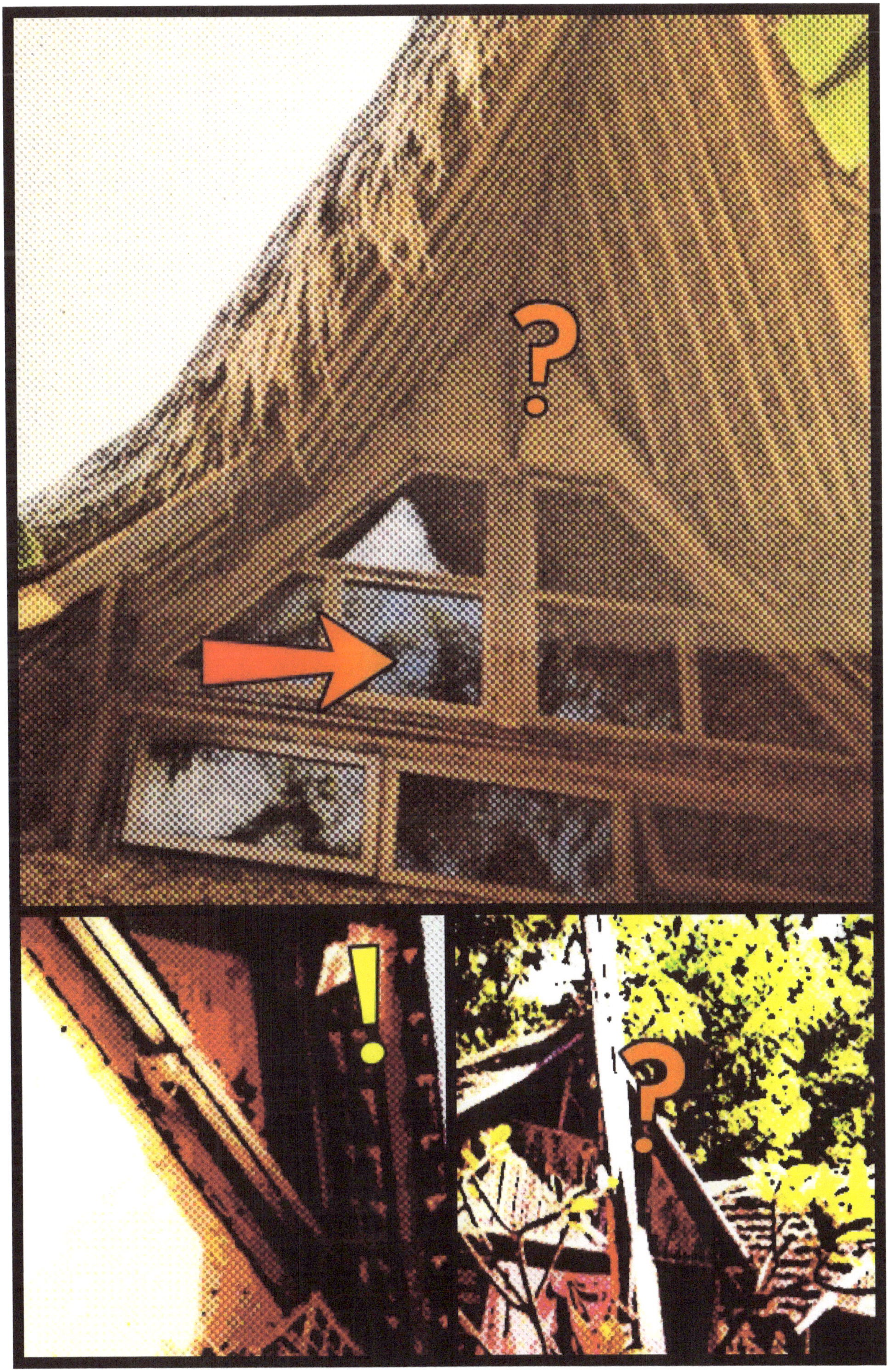

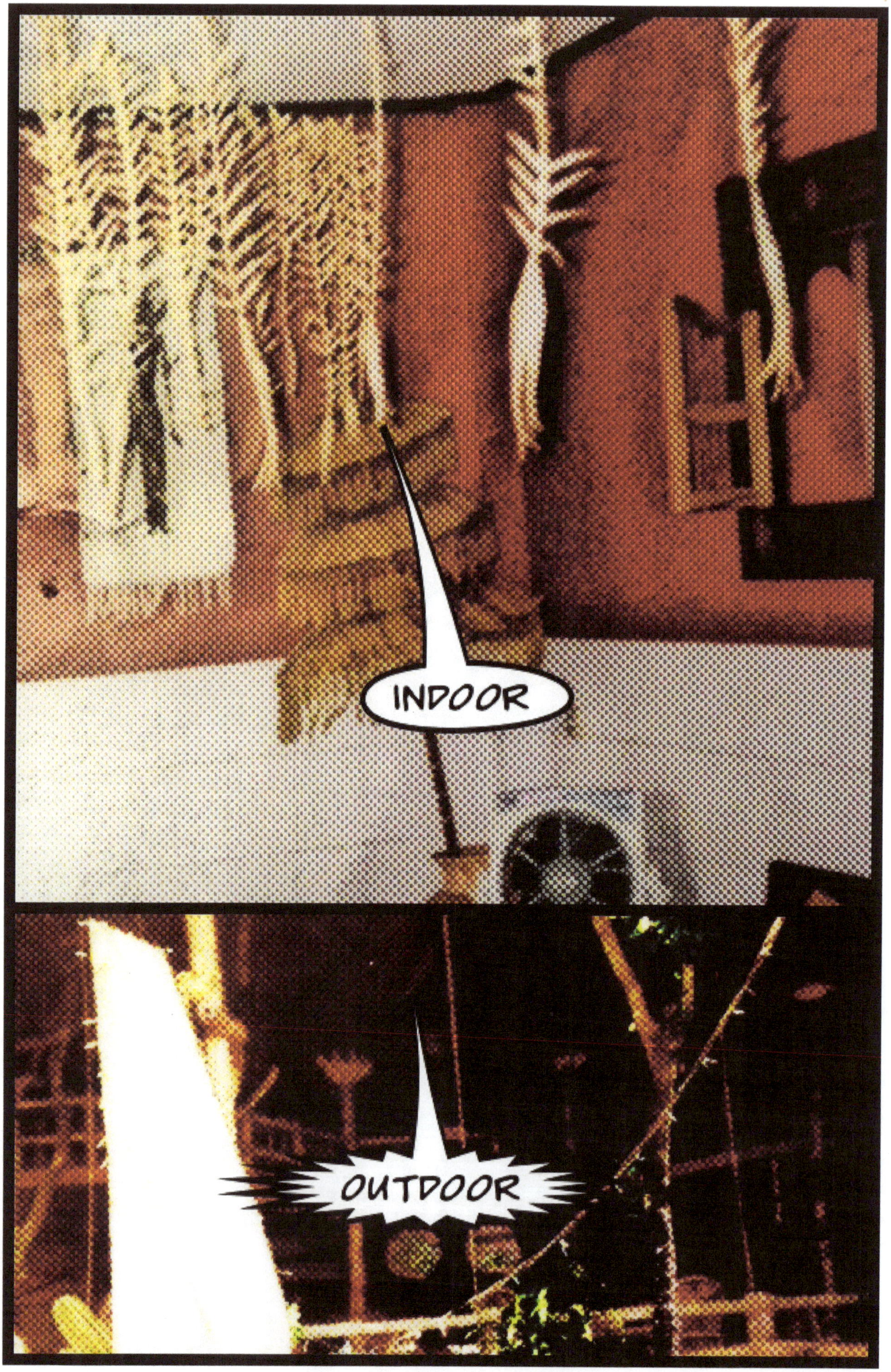
INDOOR
OUTDOOR

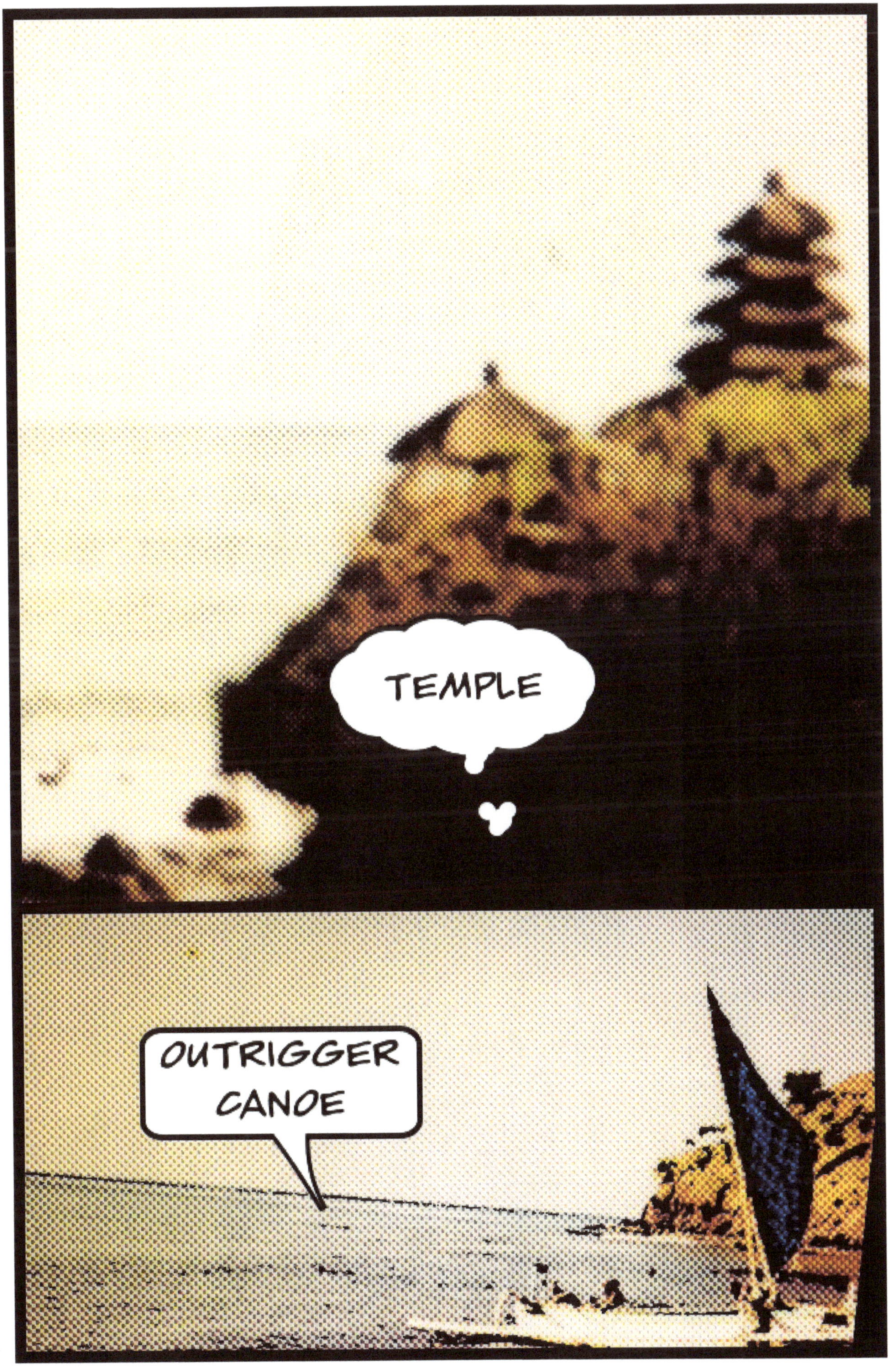
TEMPLE
OUTRIGGER CANOE

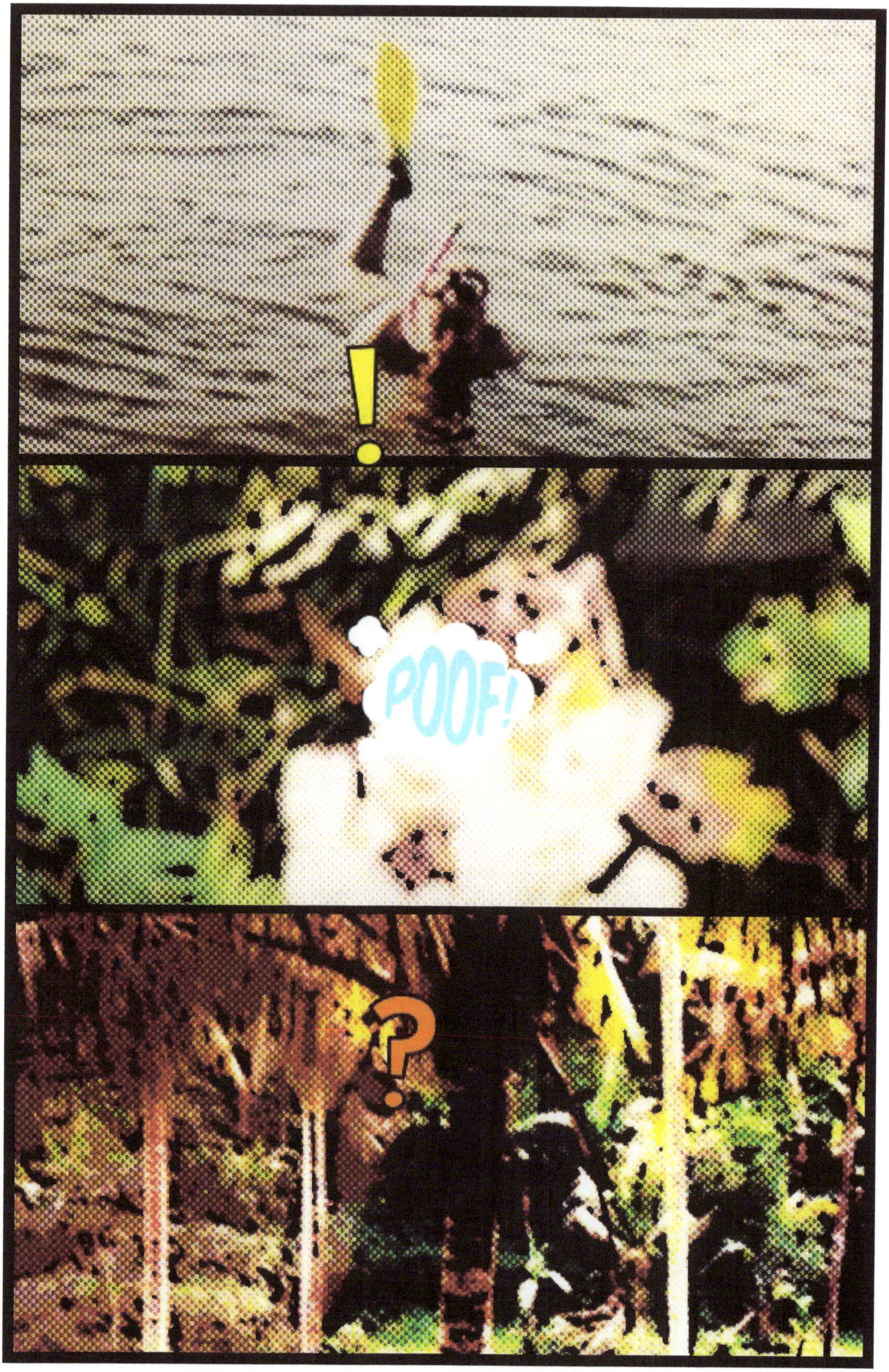
!
POOF!
?

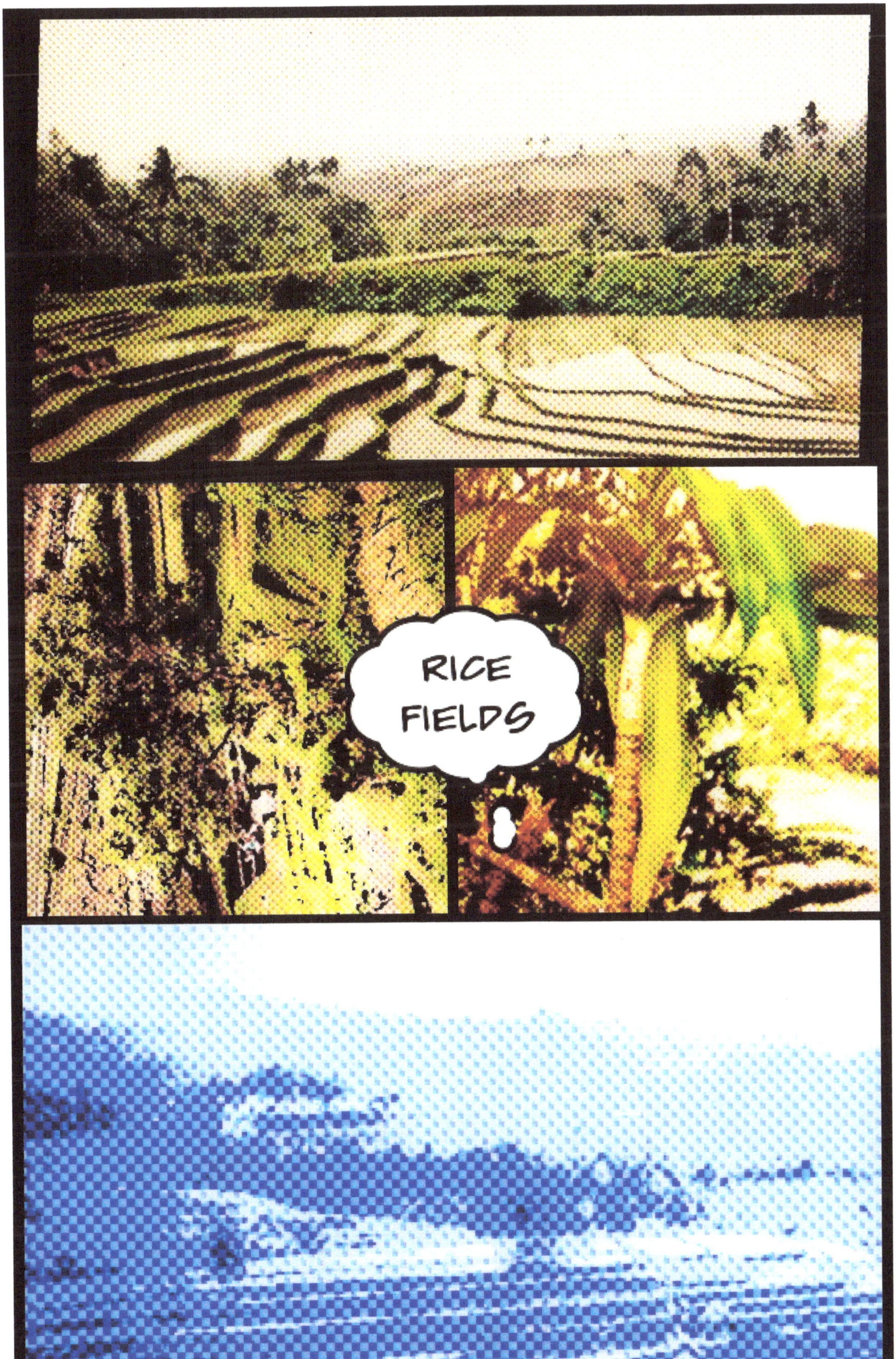
RICE FIELDS

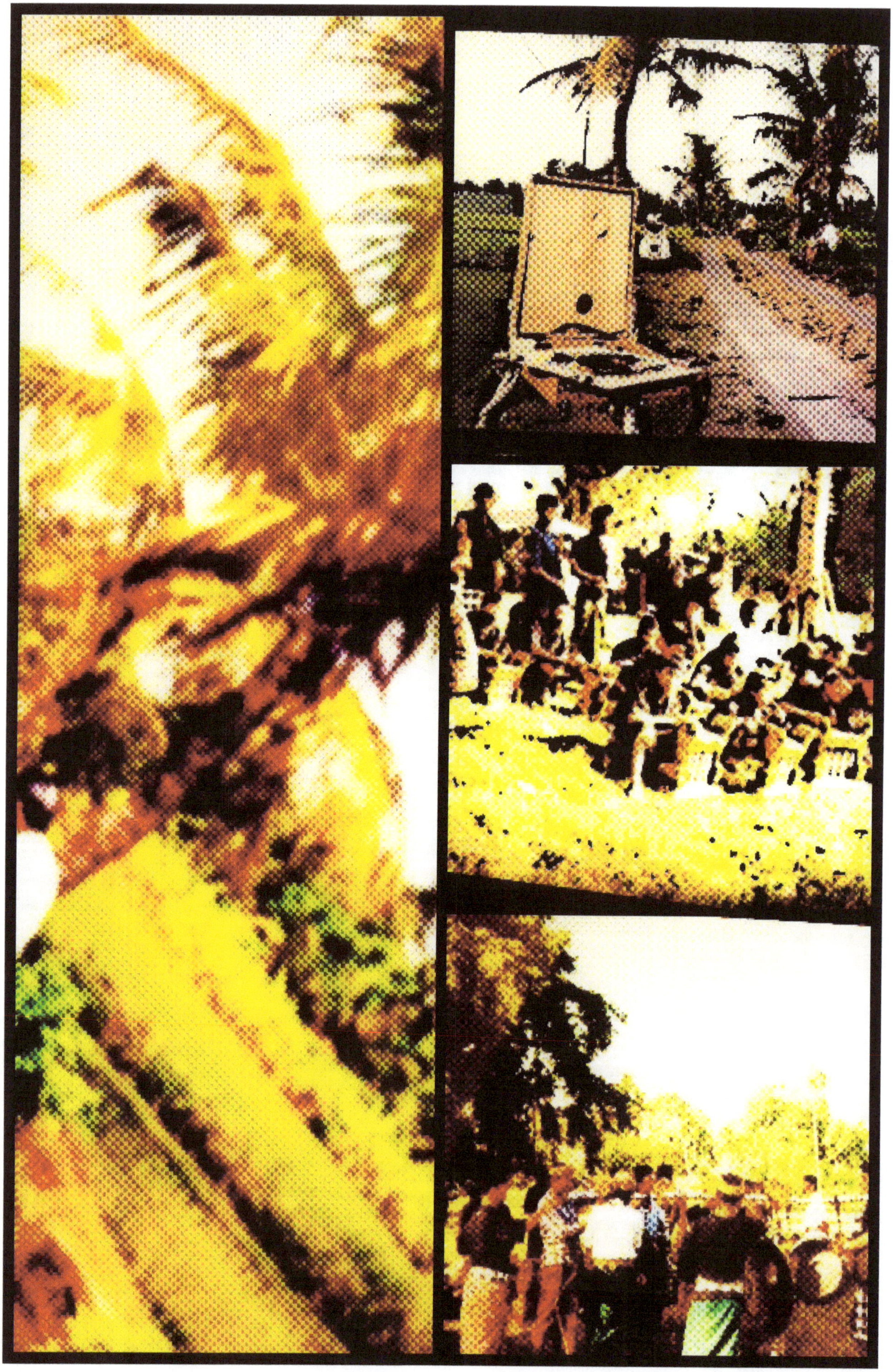

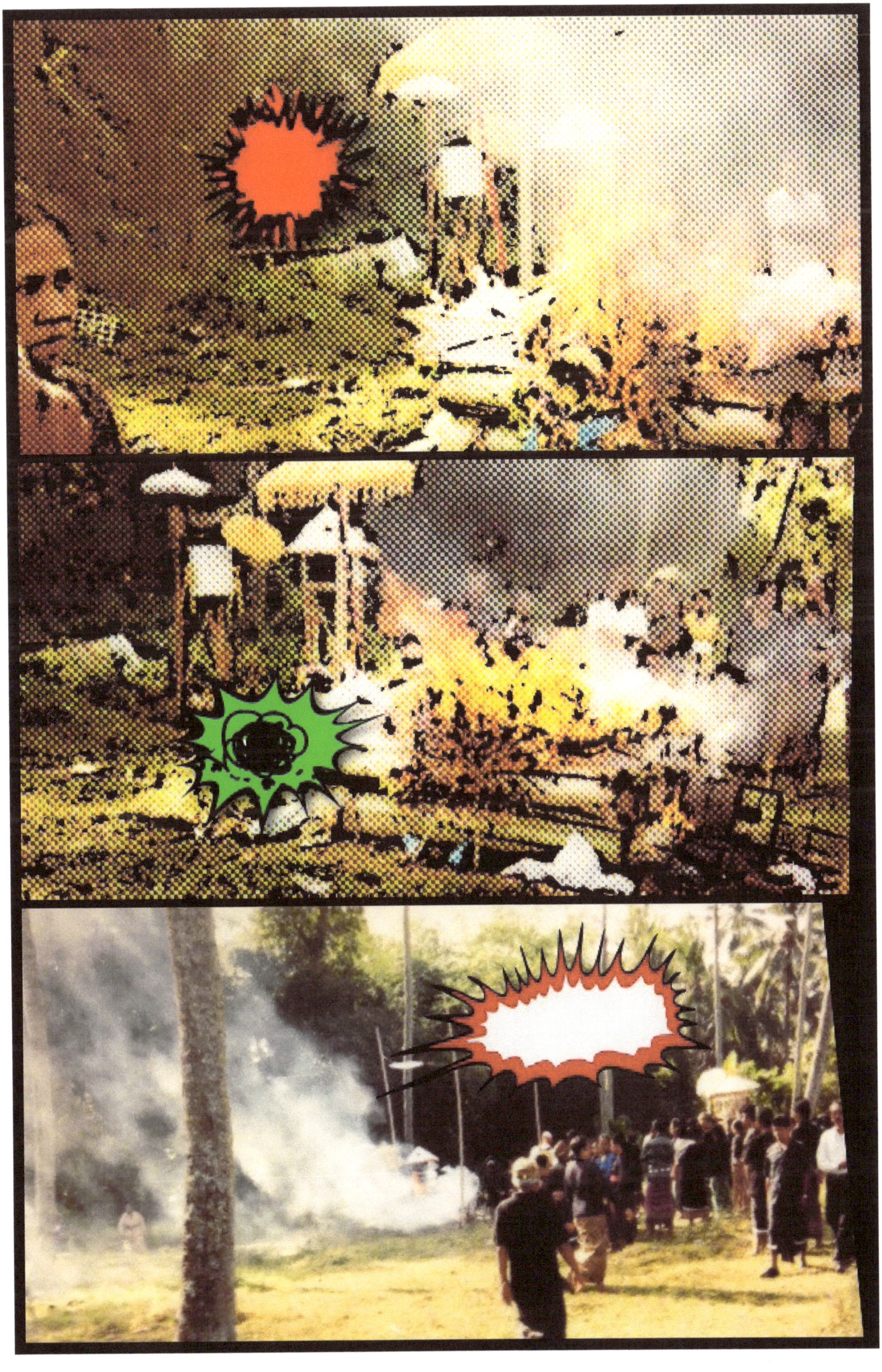

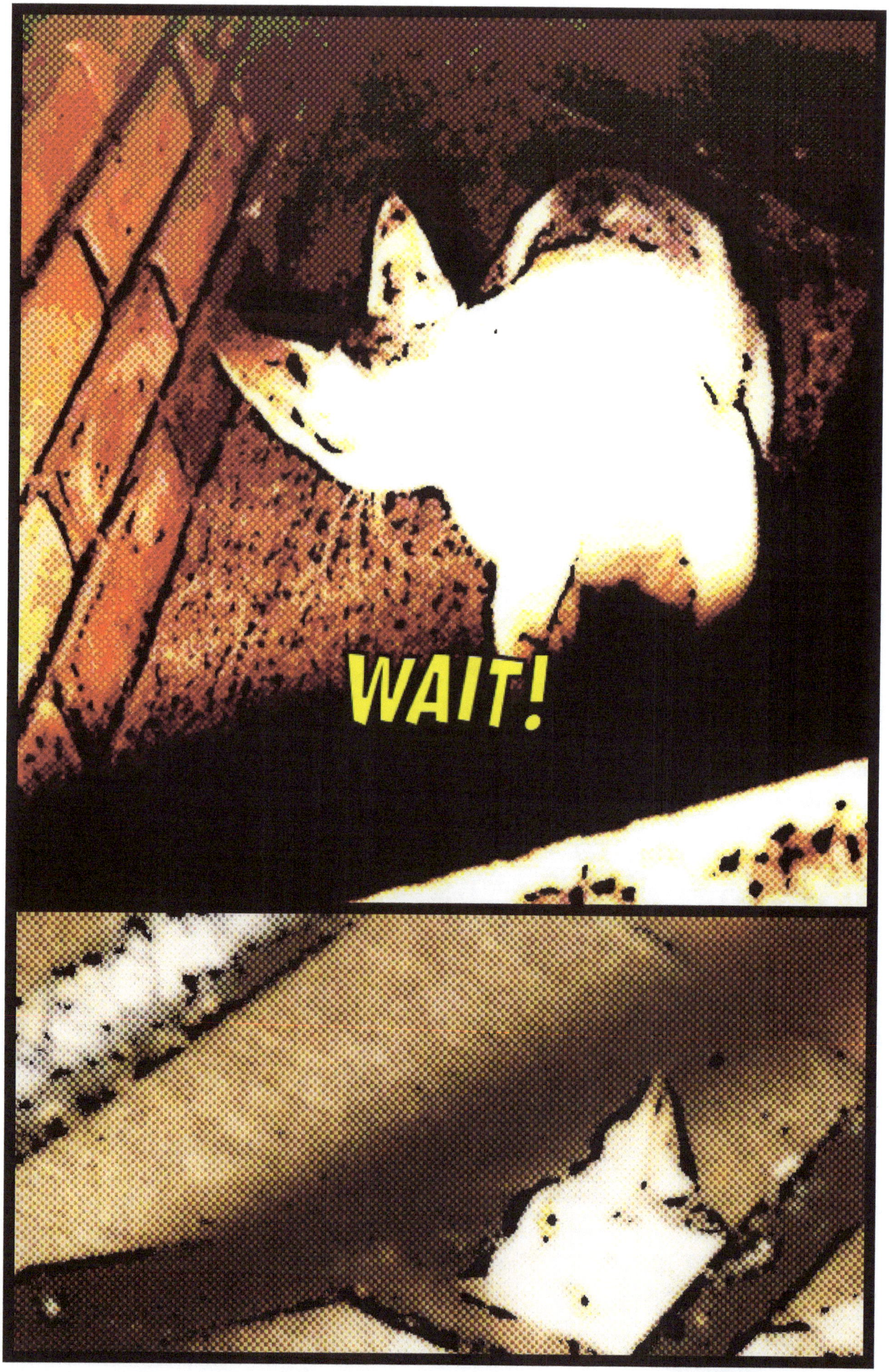
WAIT!

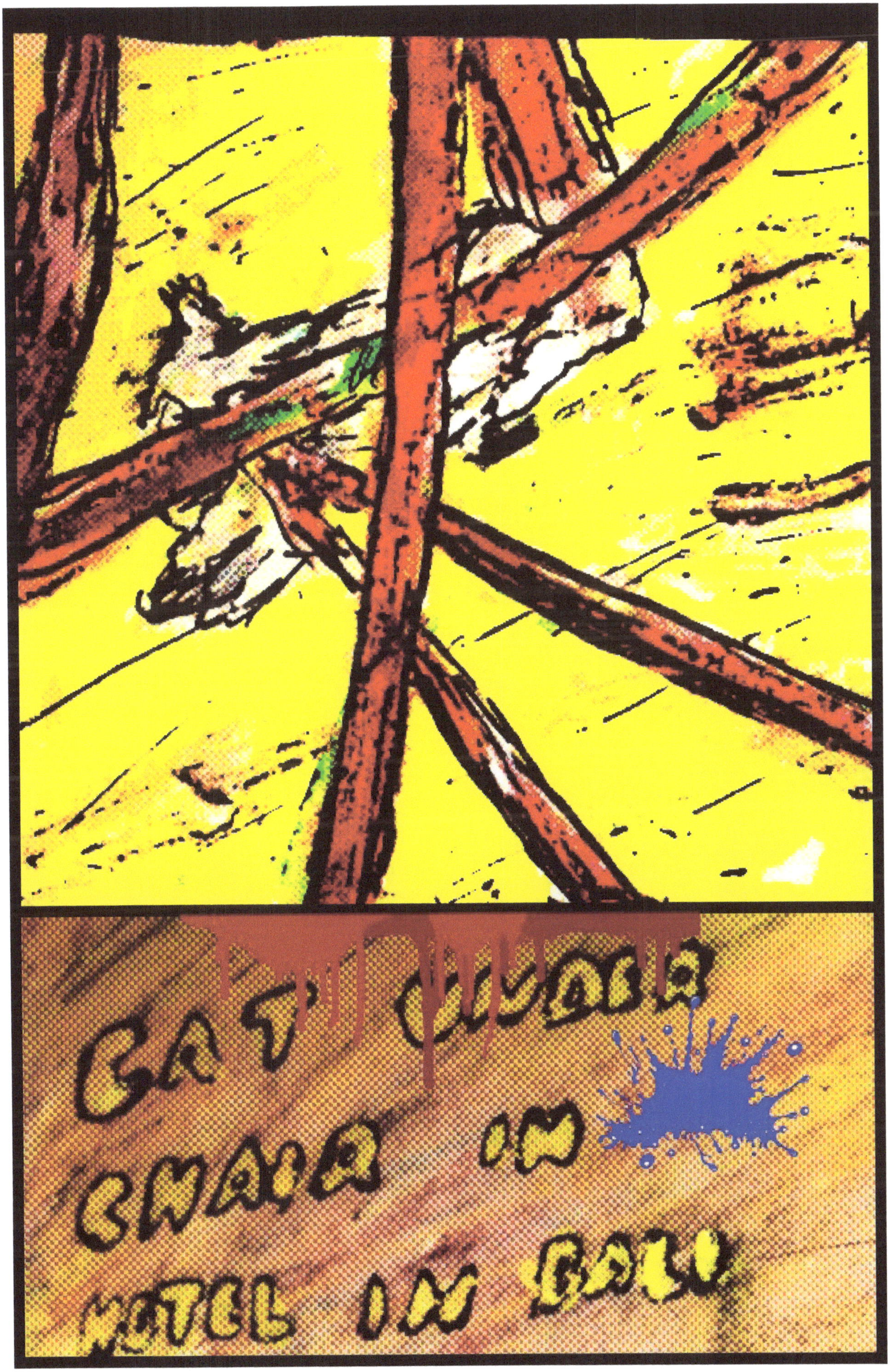
CAT UNDER
CHAIR IN
HOTEL IN BALI

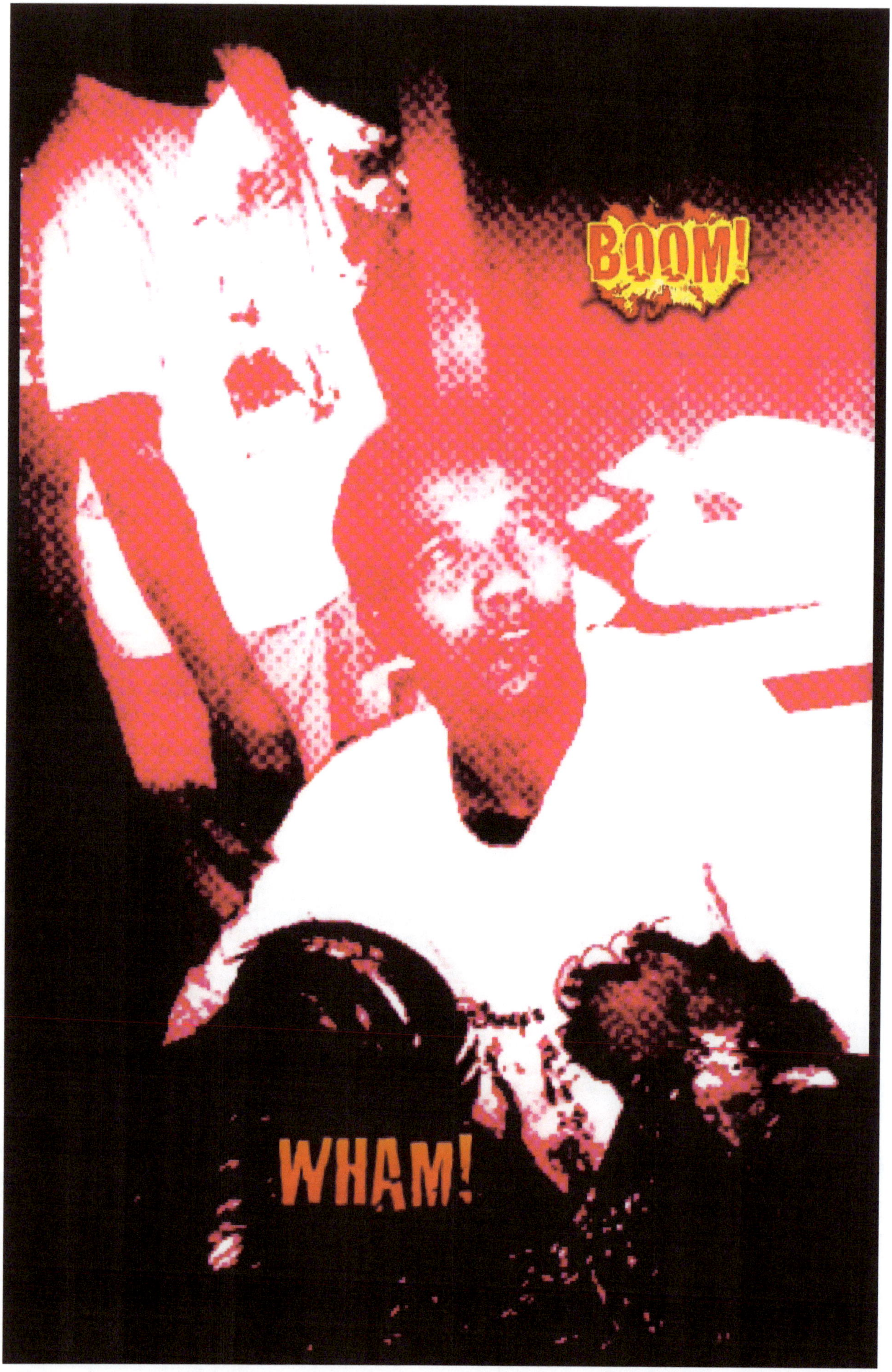
BOOM!
WHAM!

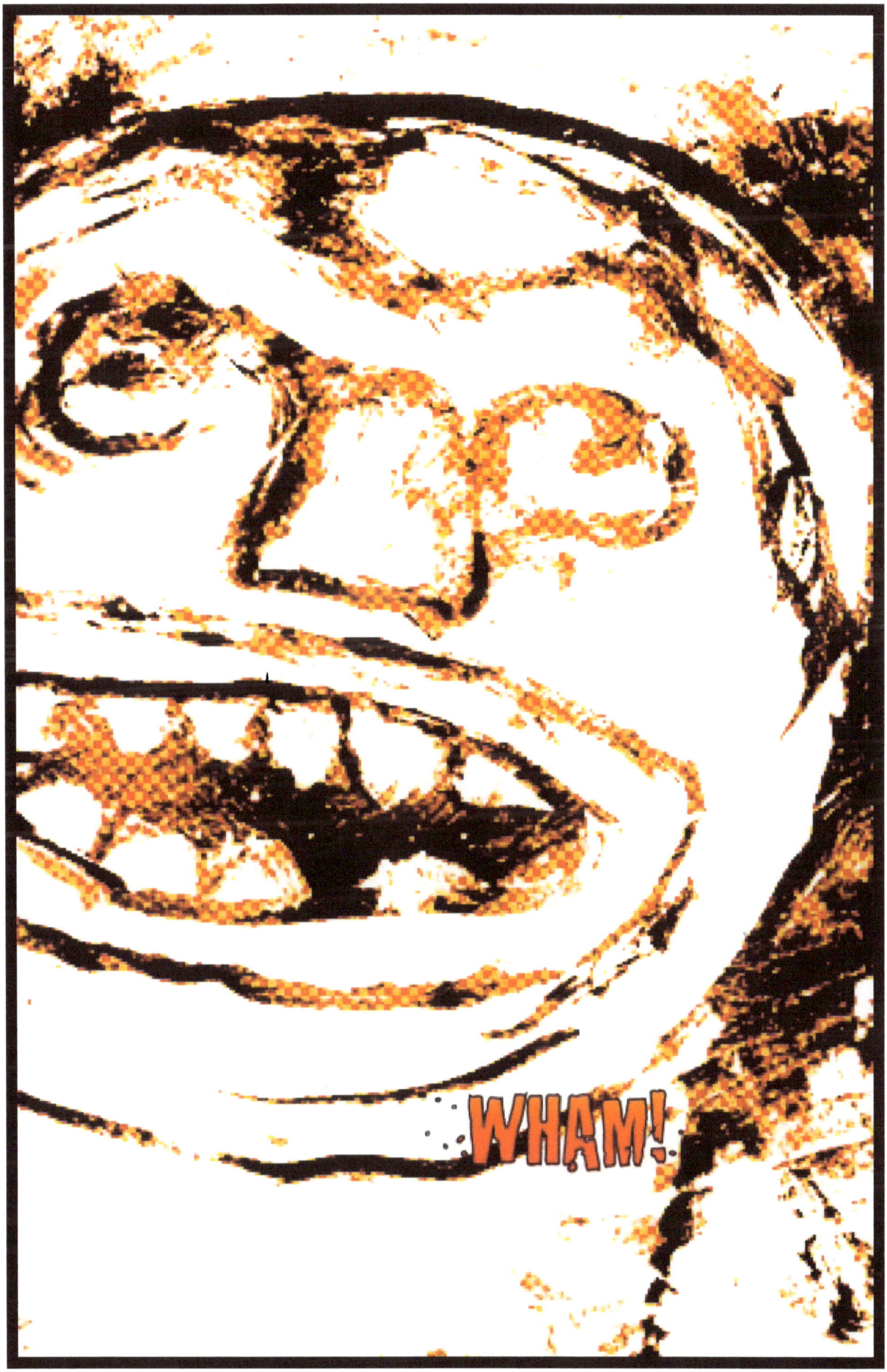
WHAM!

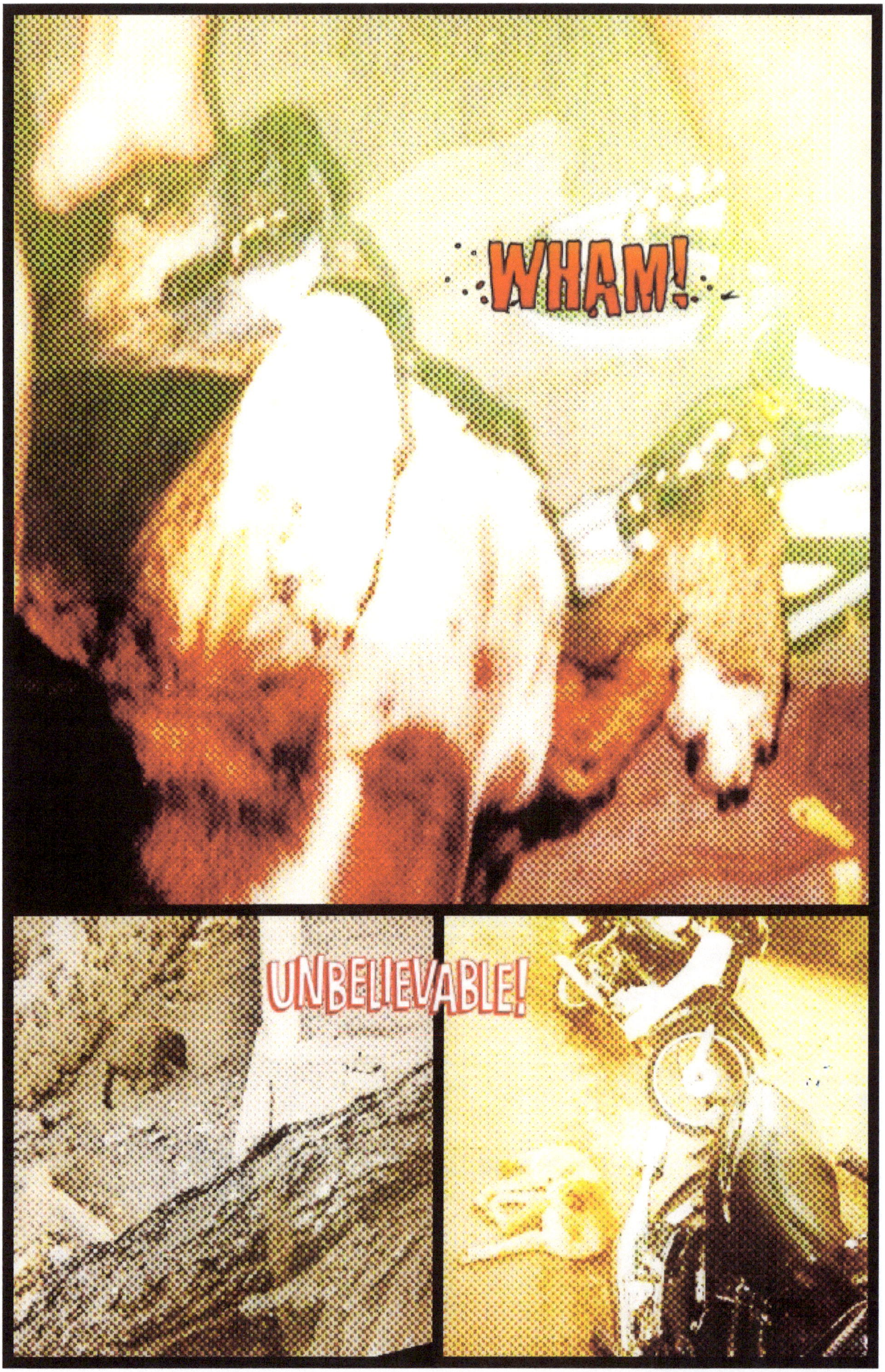
WHAM!
UNBELIEVABLE!

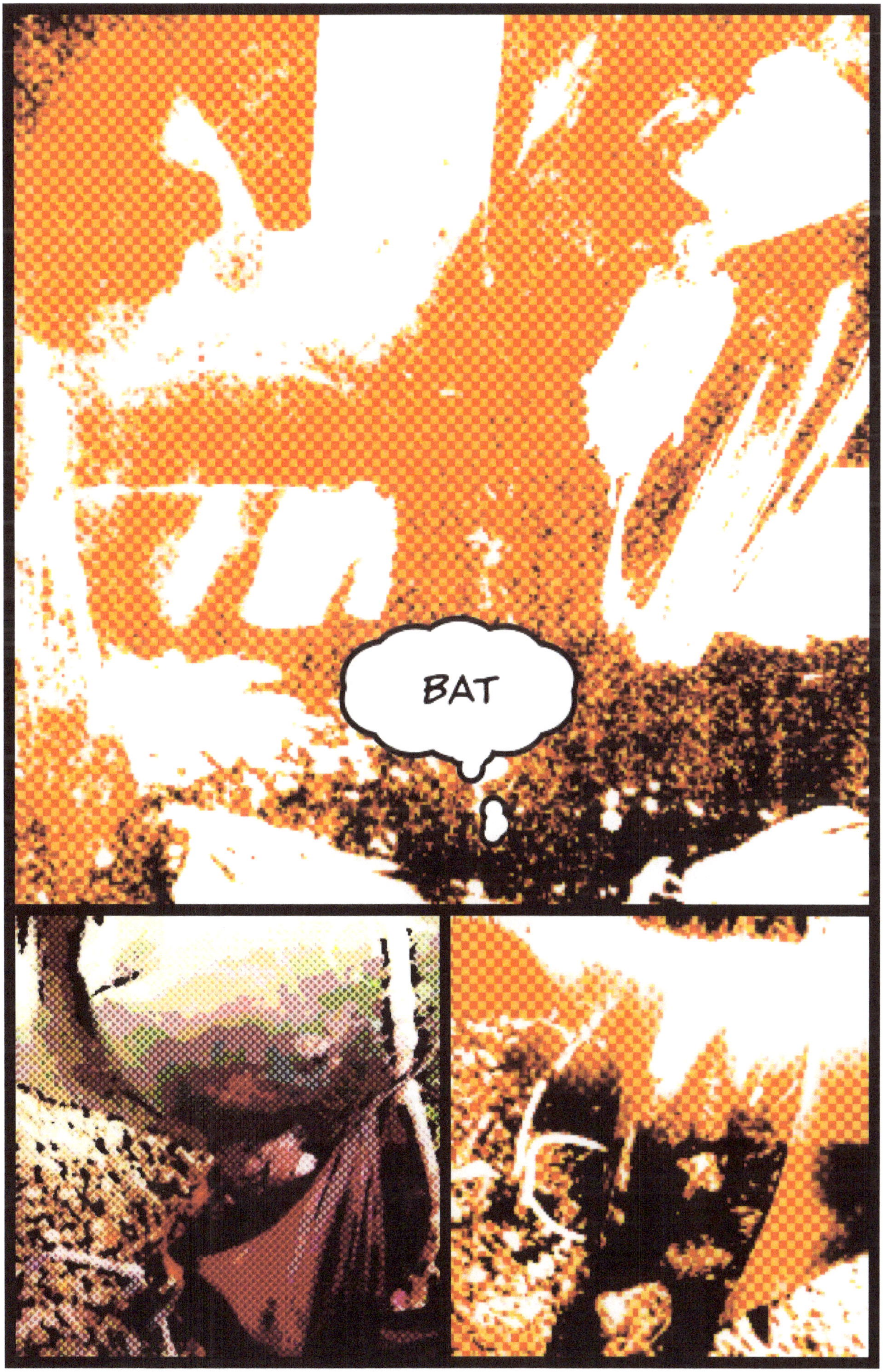
BAT

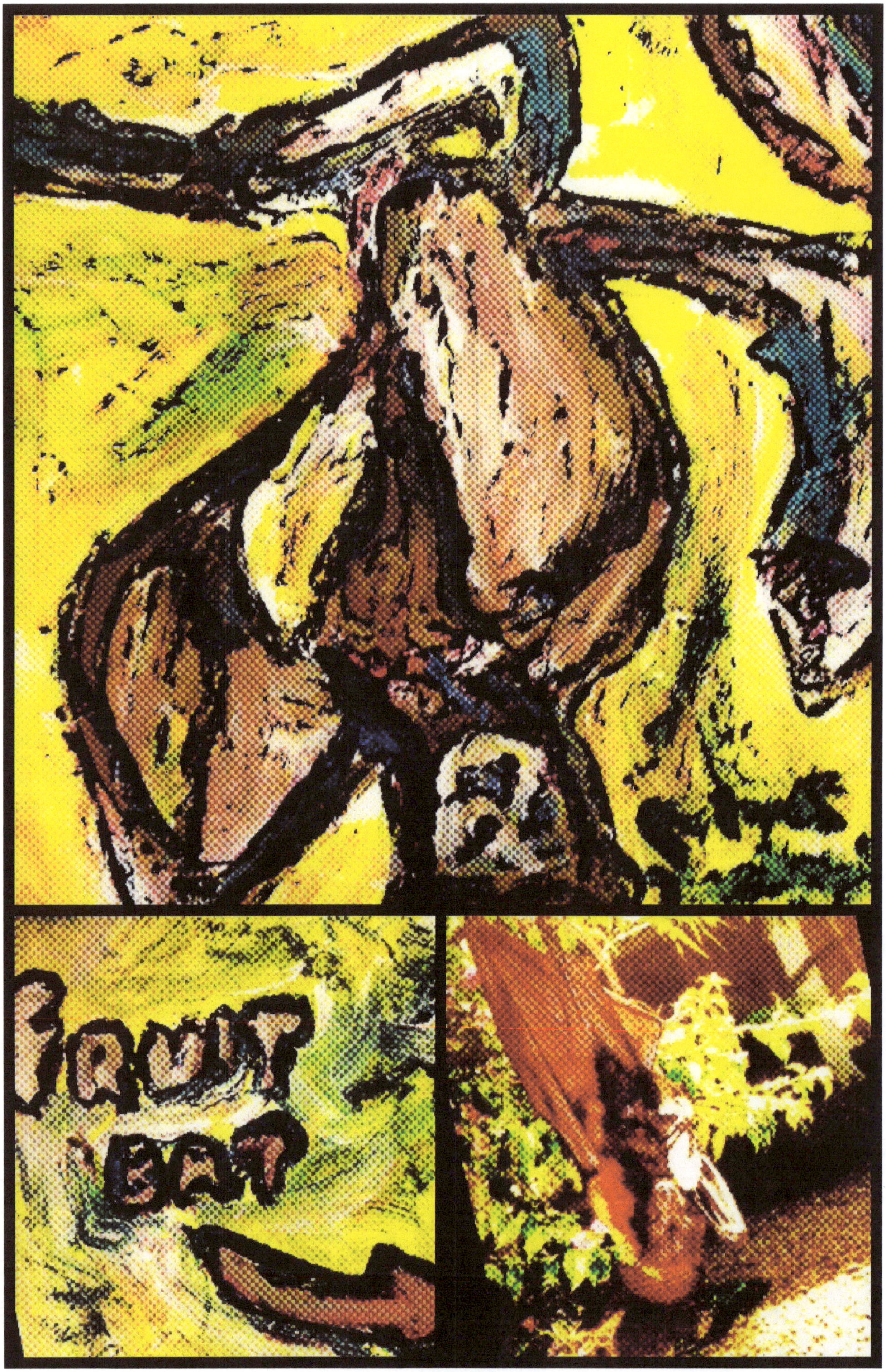
FRUIT
BAT

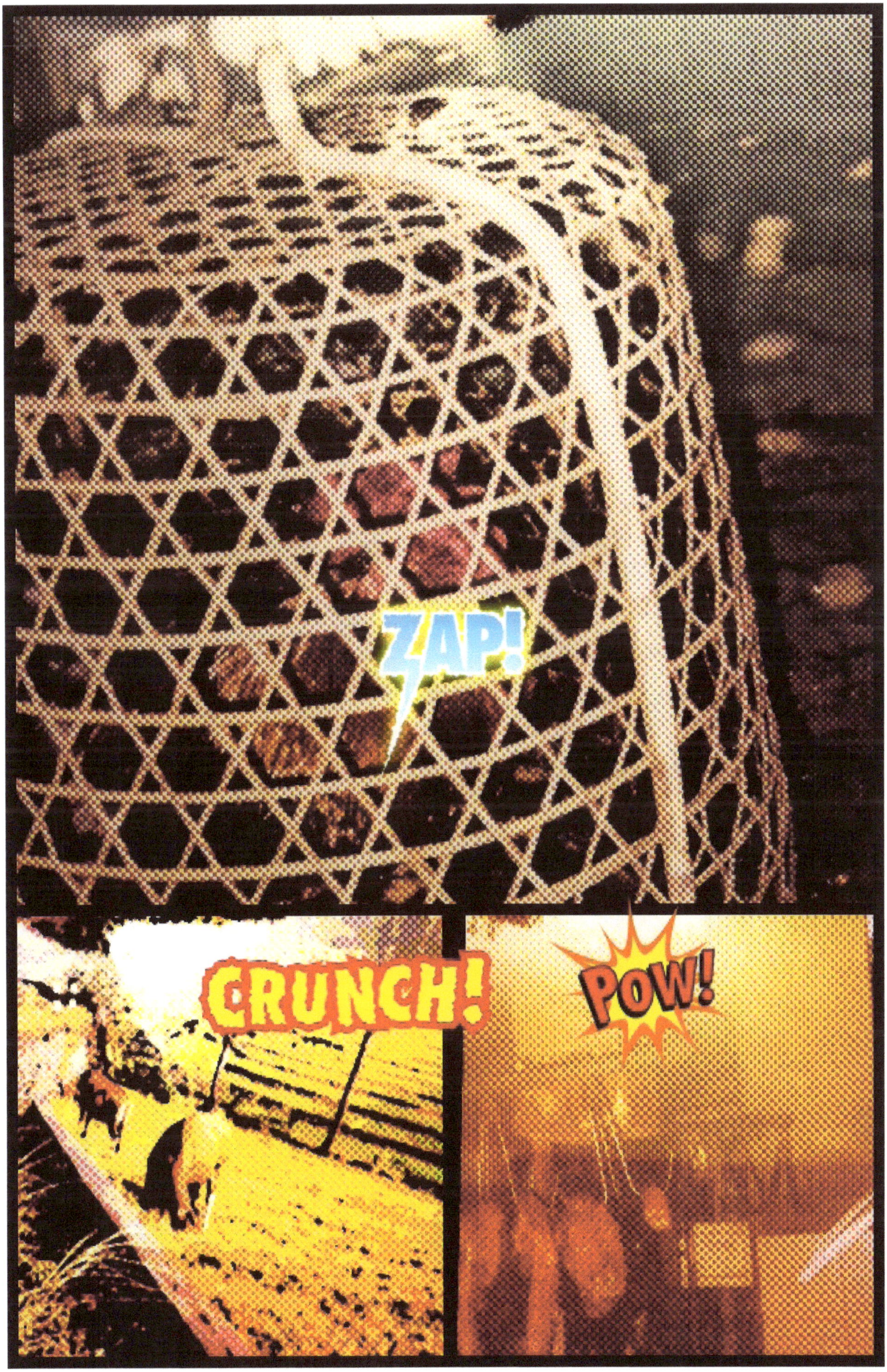
ZAP!
CRUNCH!
POW!

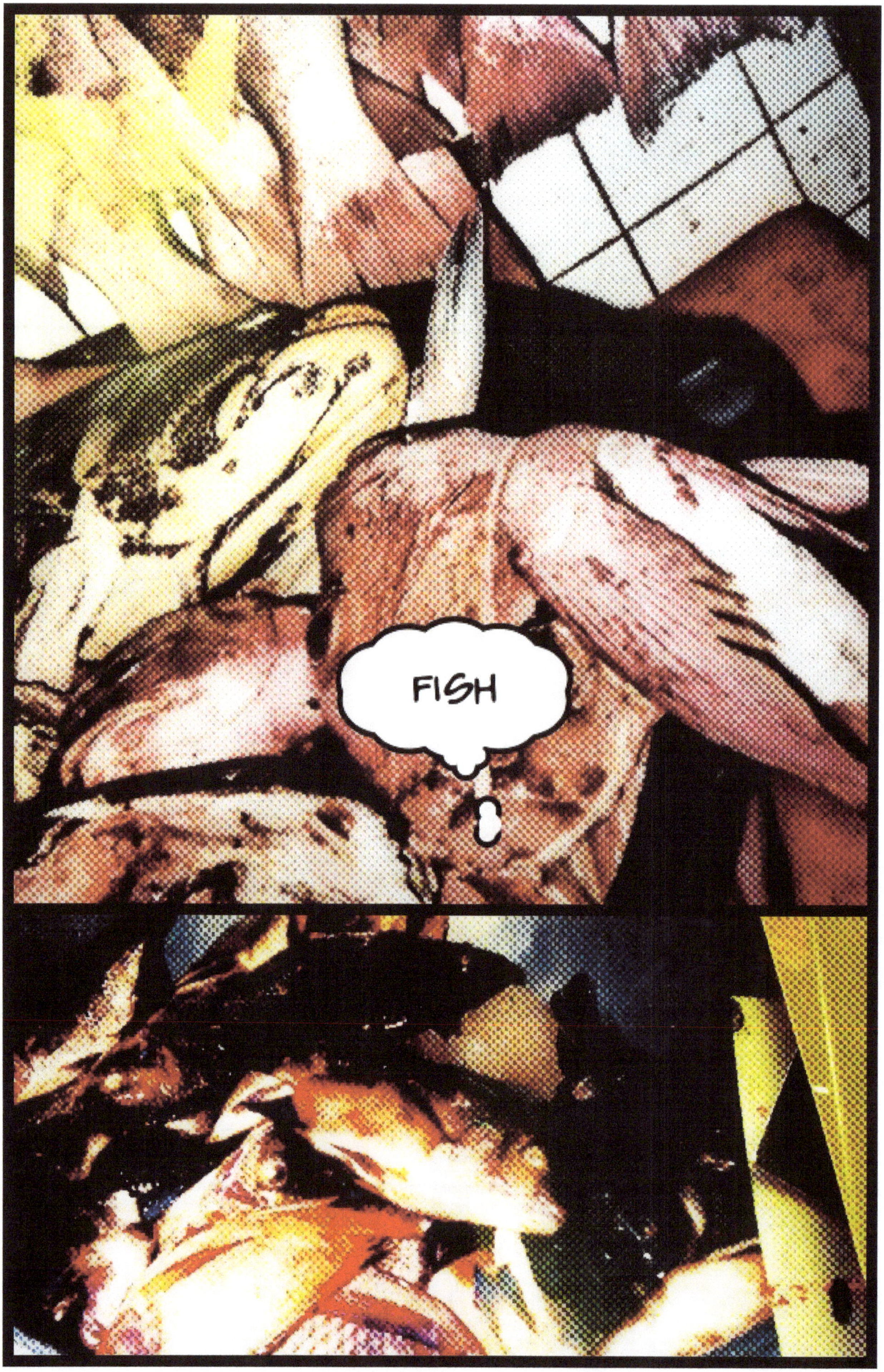
FISH

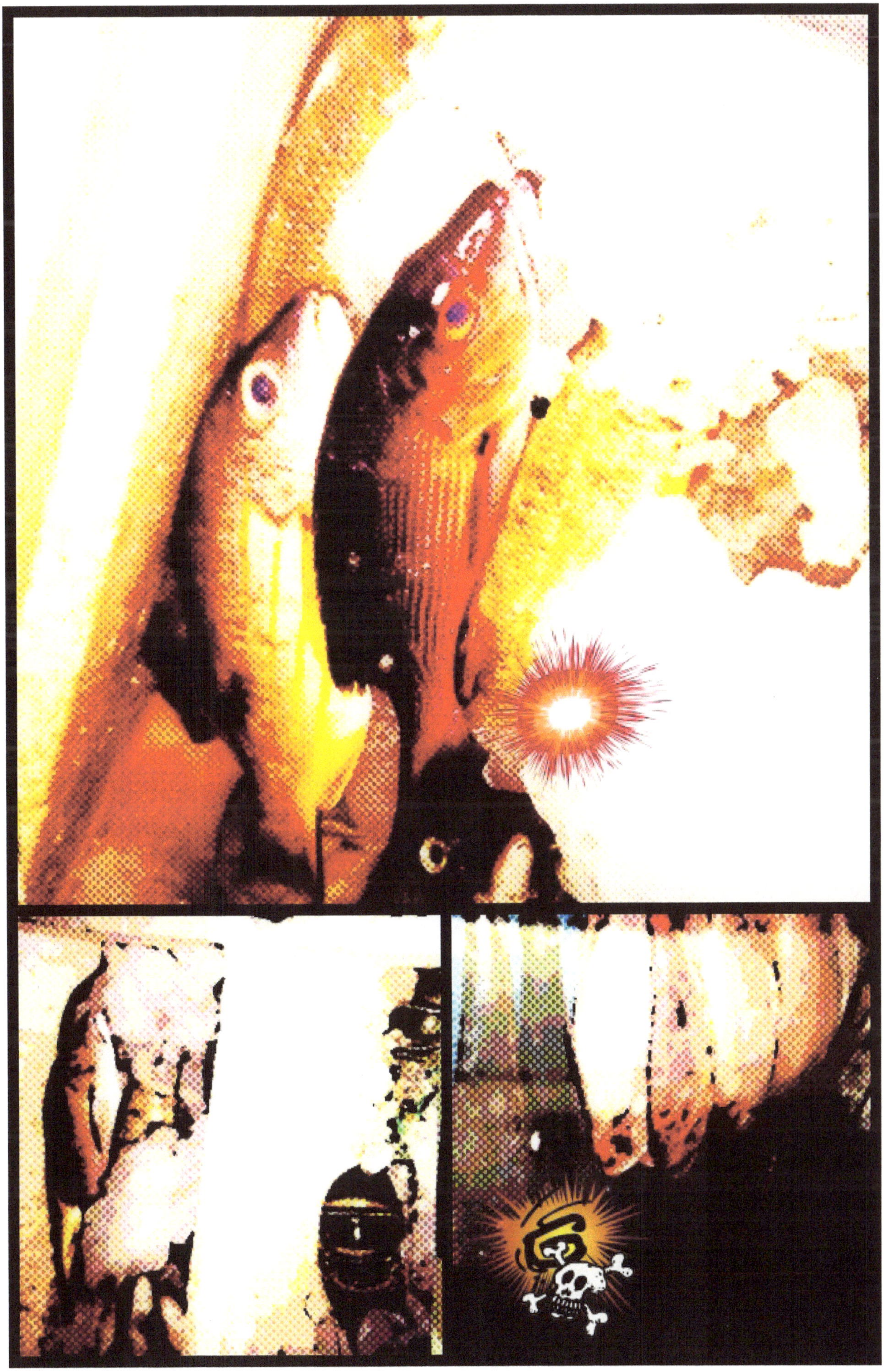

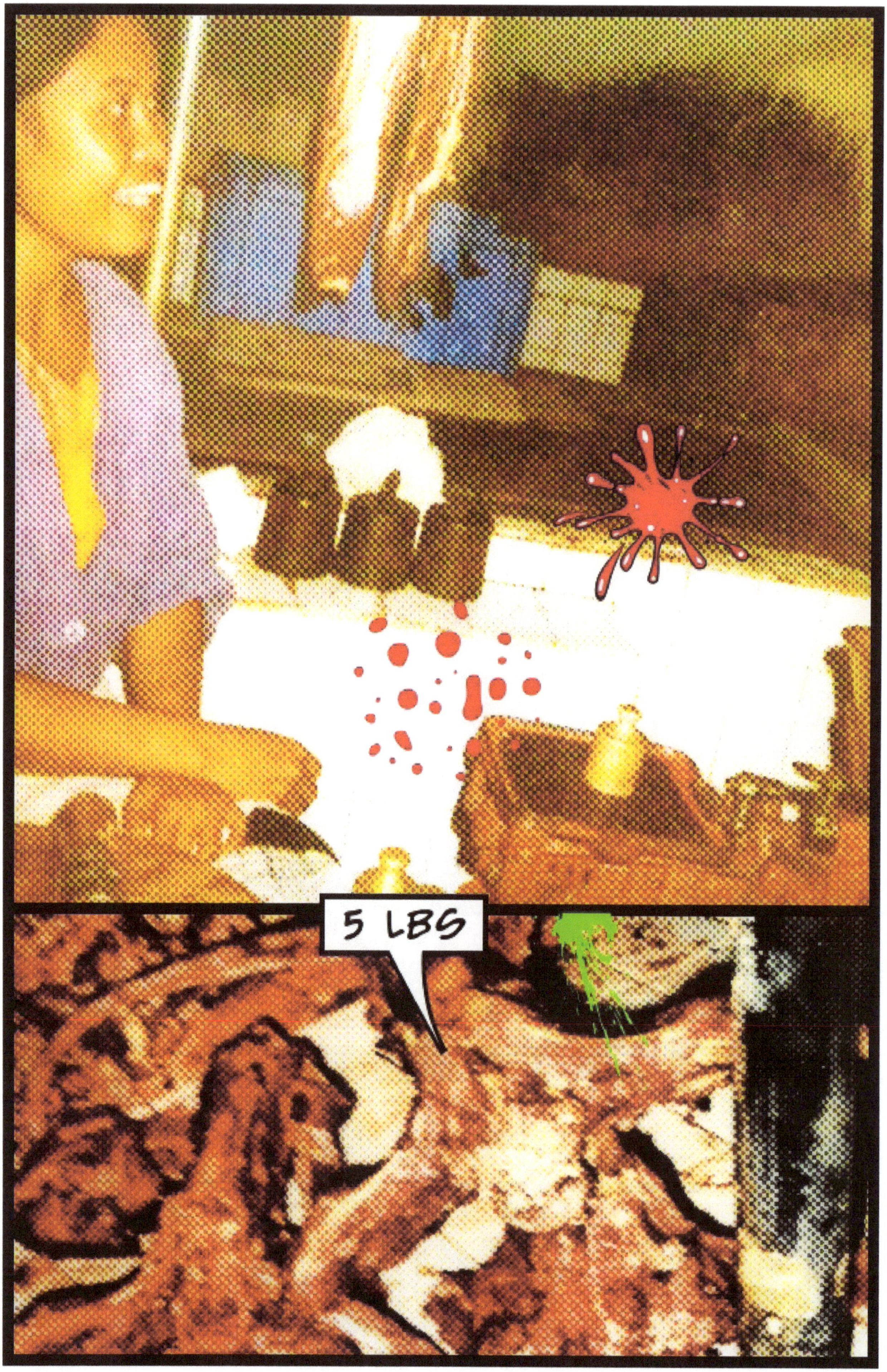
5 LBS

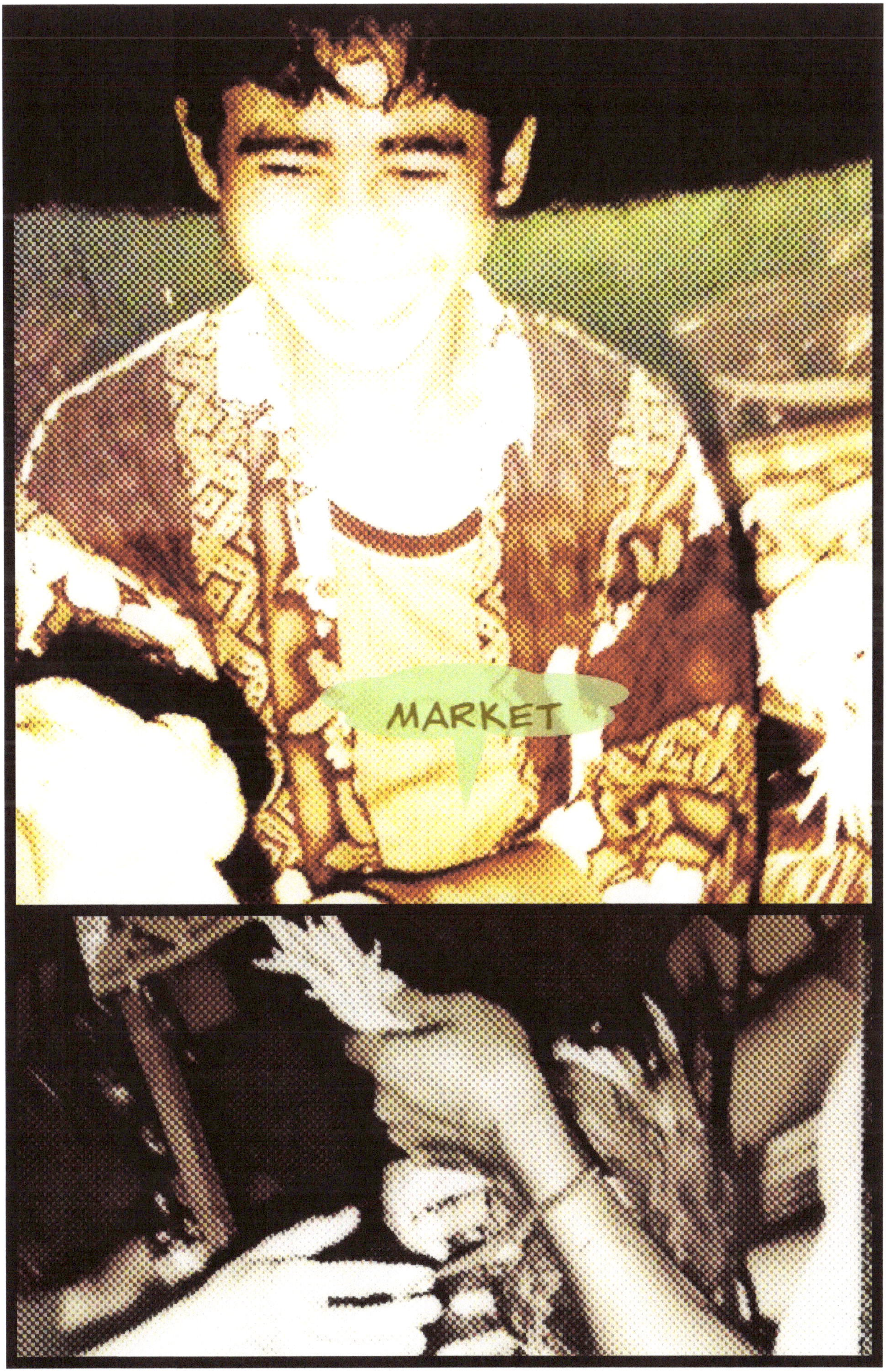
MARKET

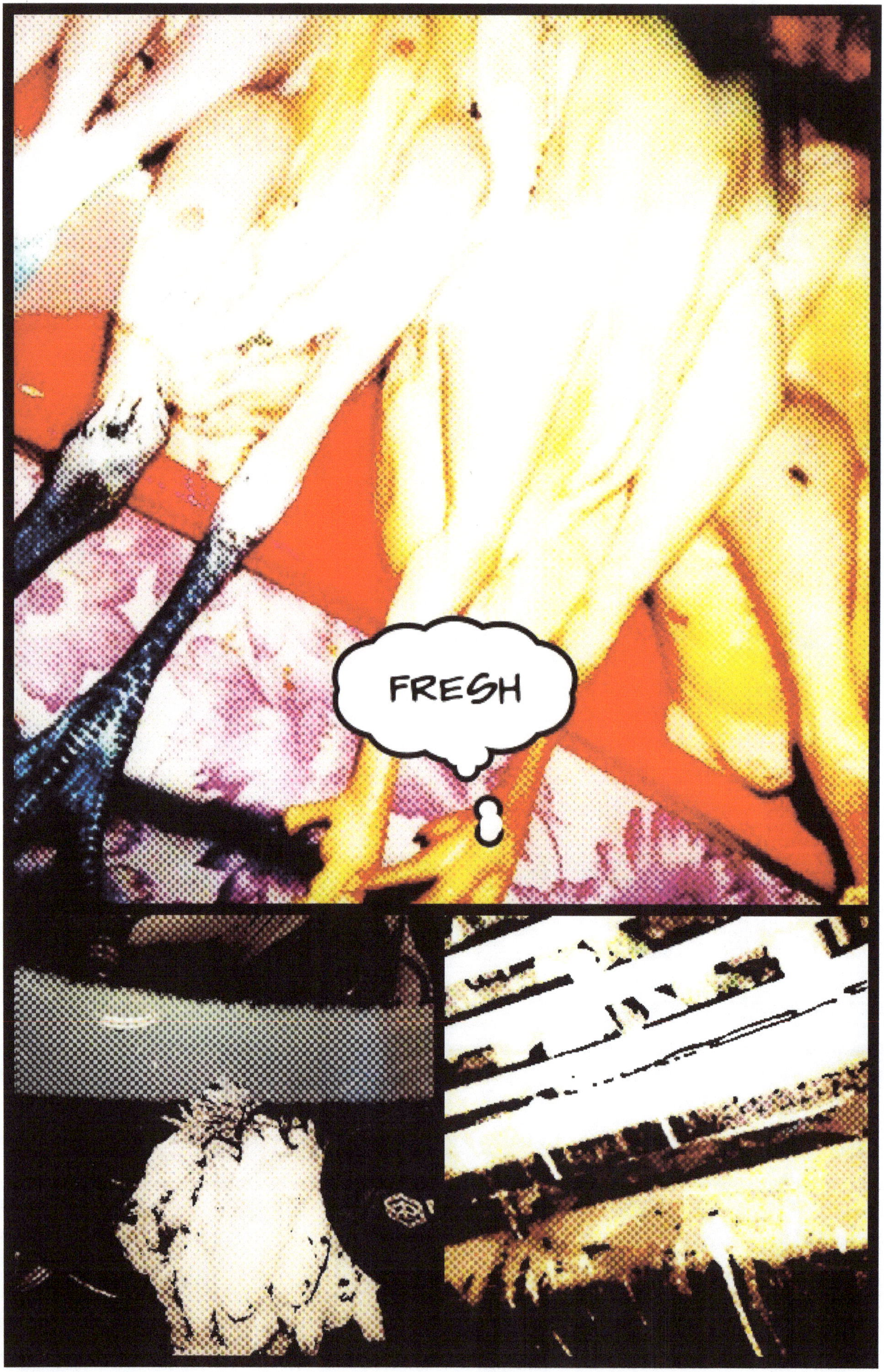
FRESH

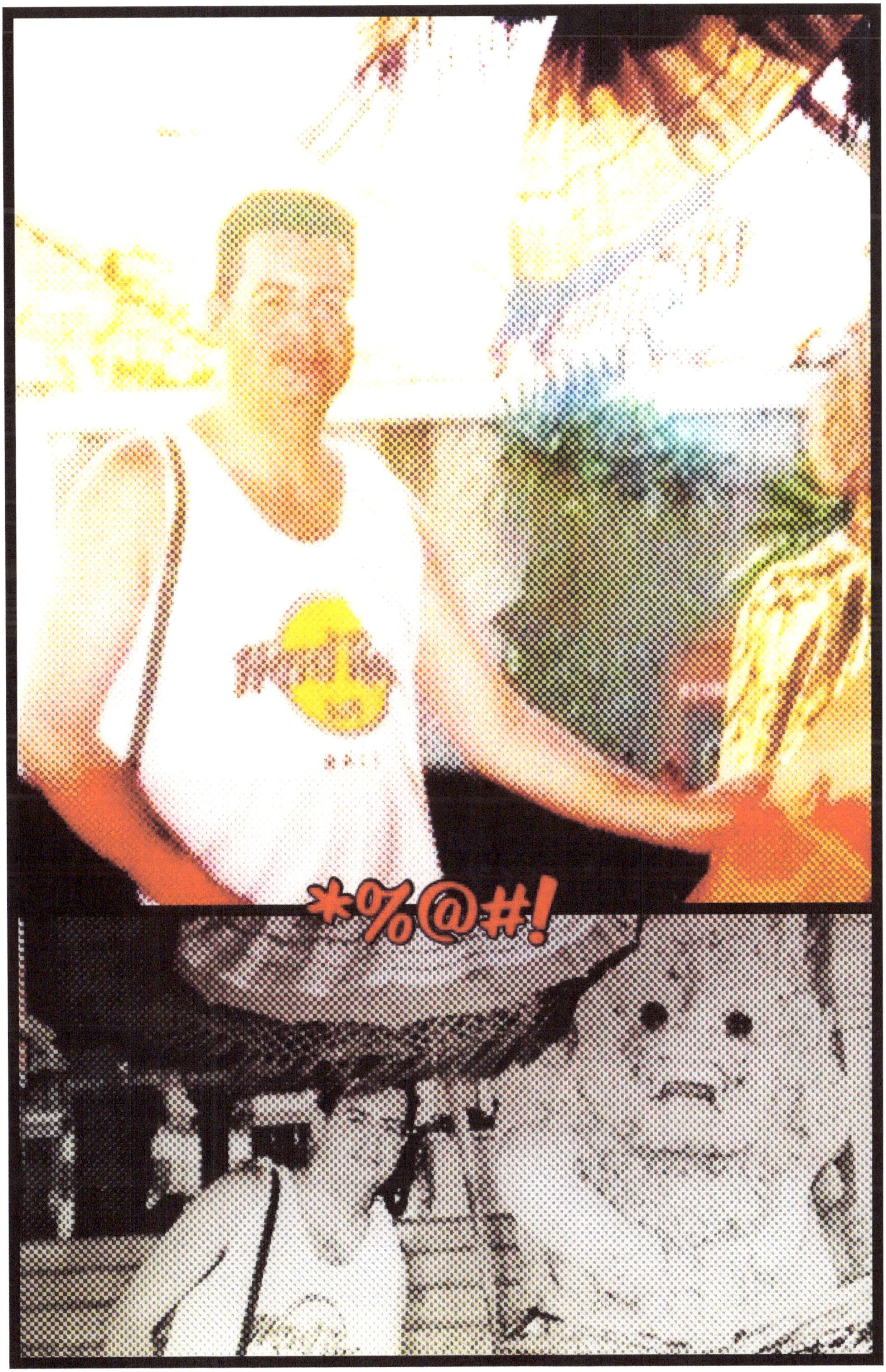

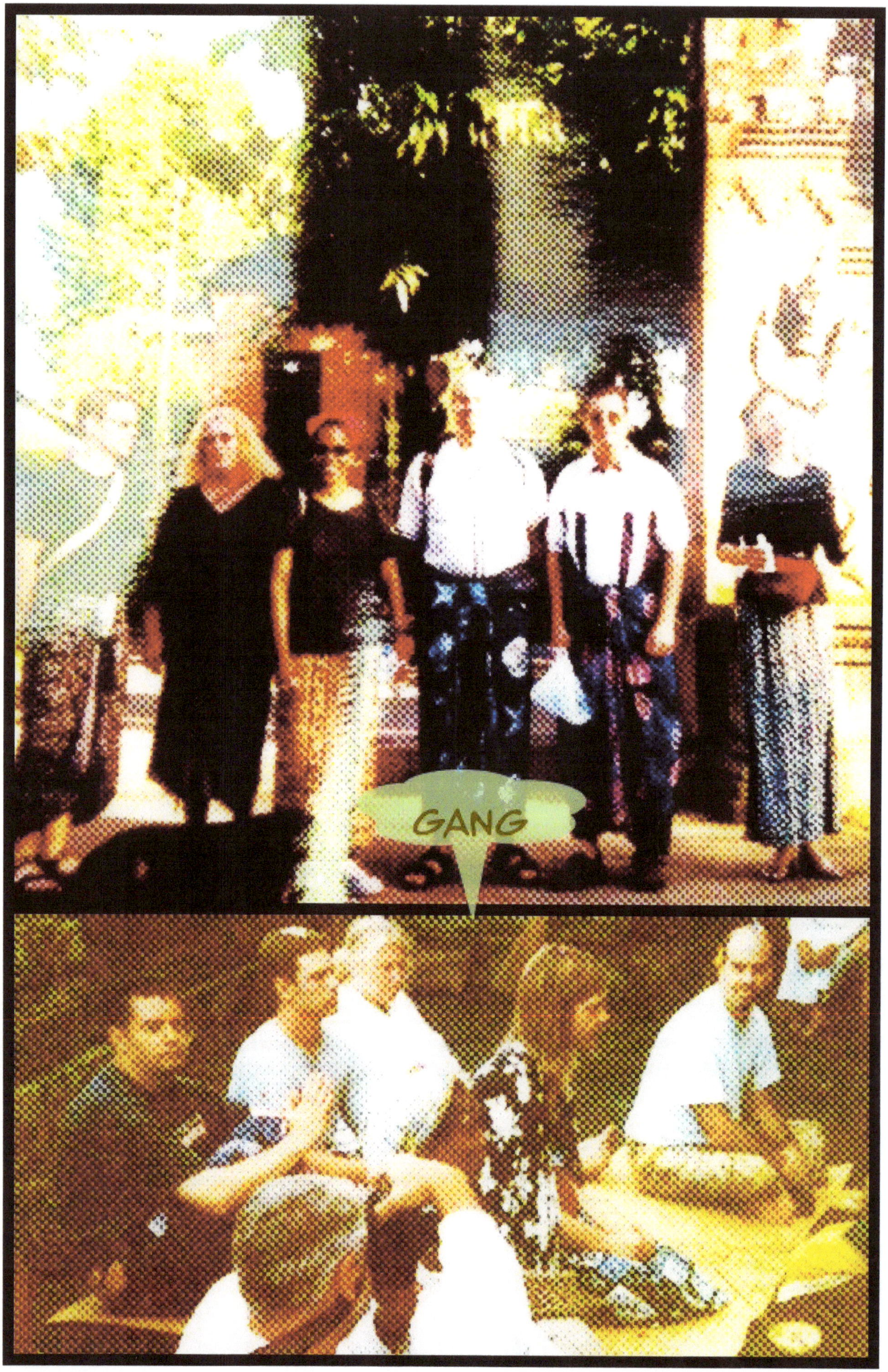
GANG

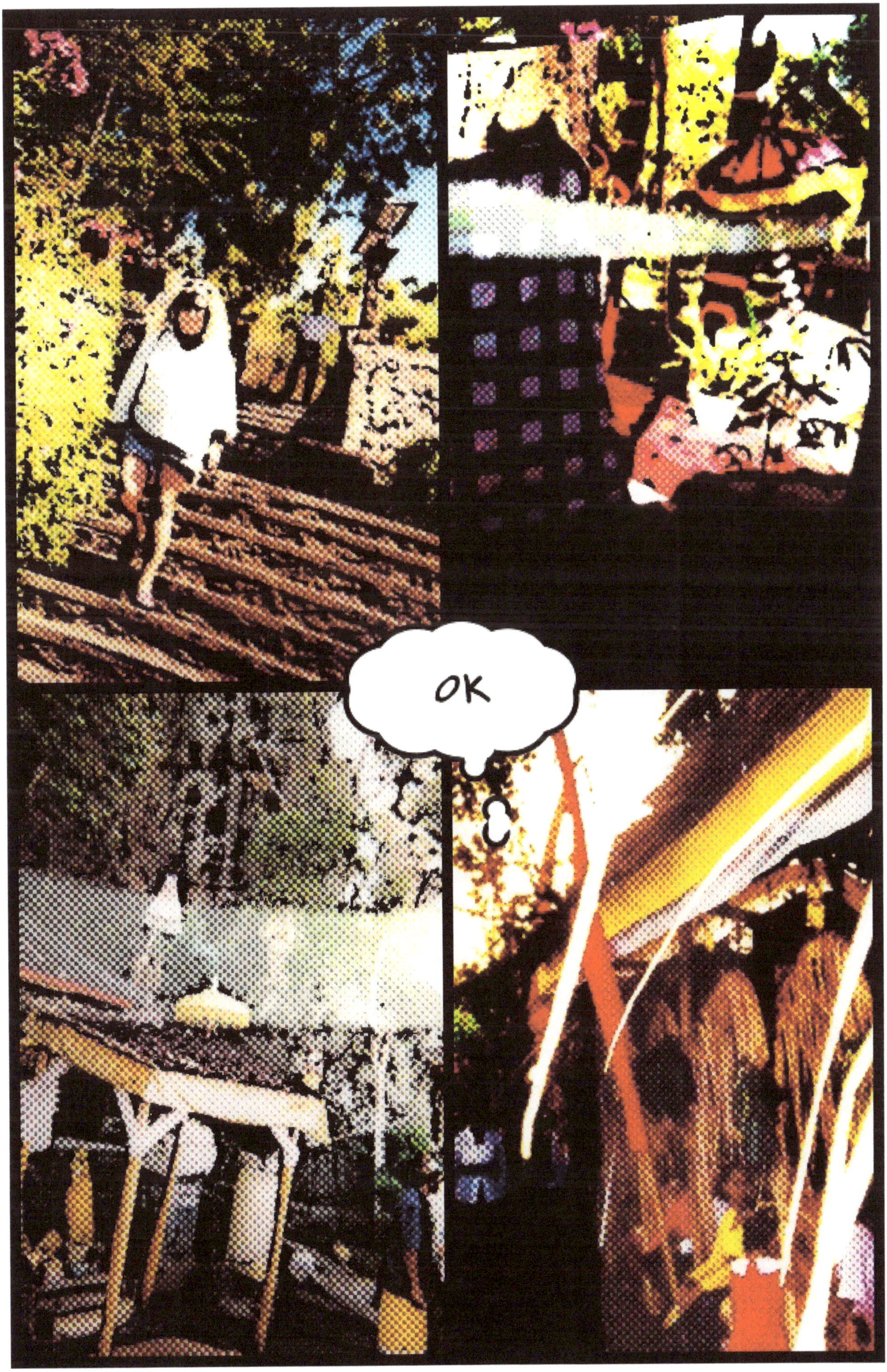
OK

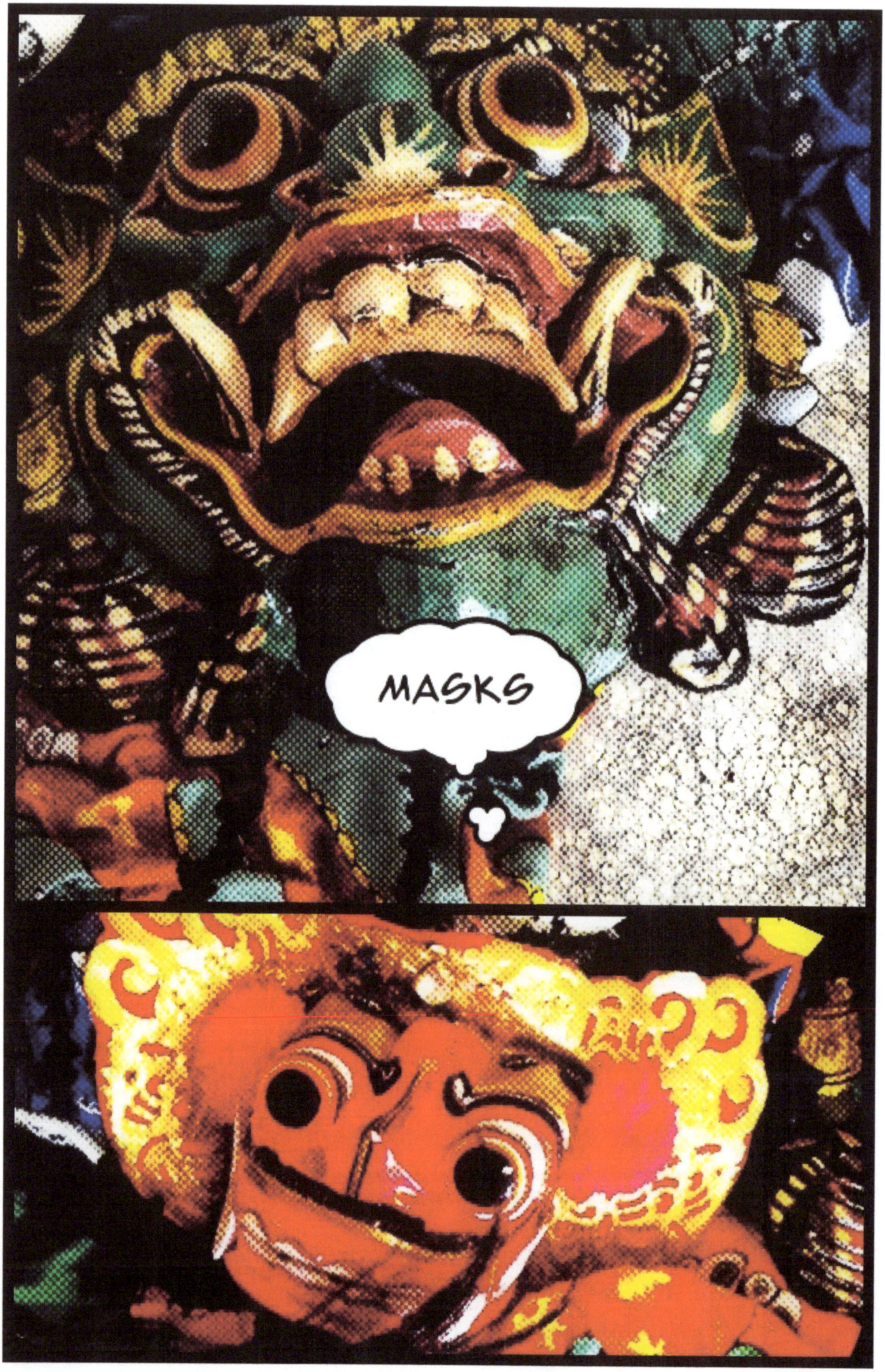
MASKS

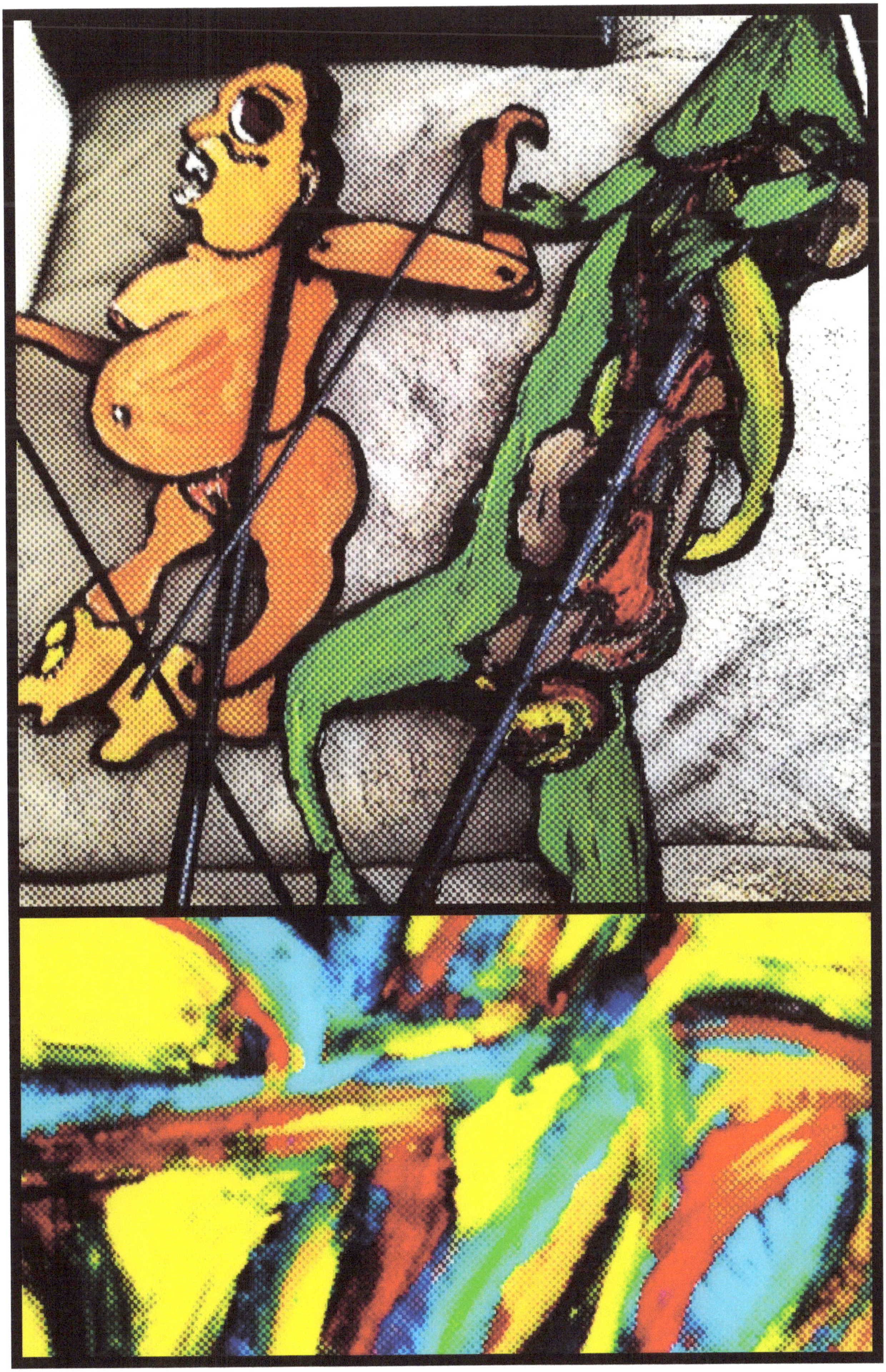

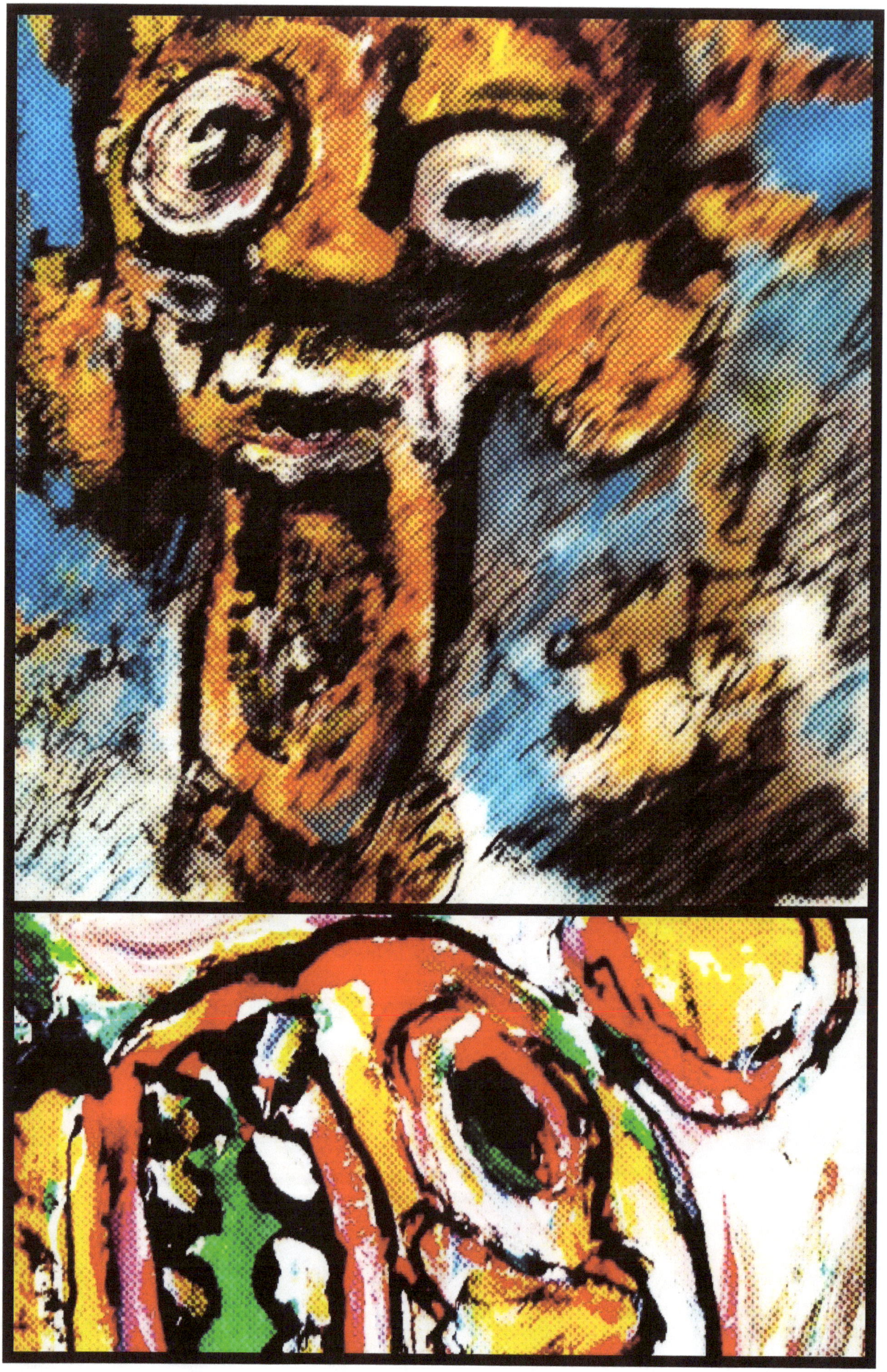

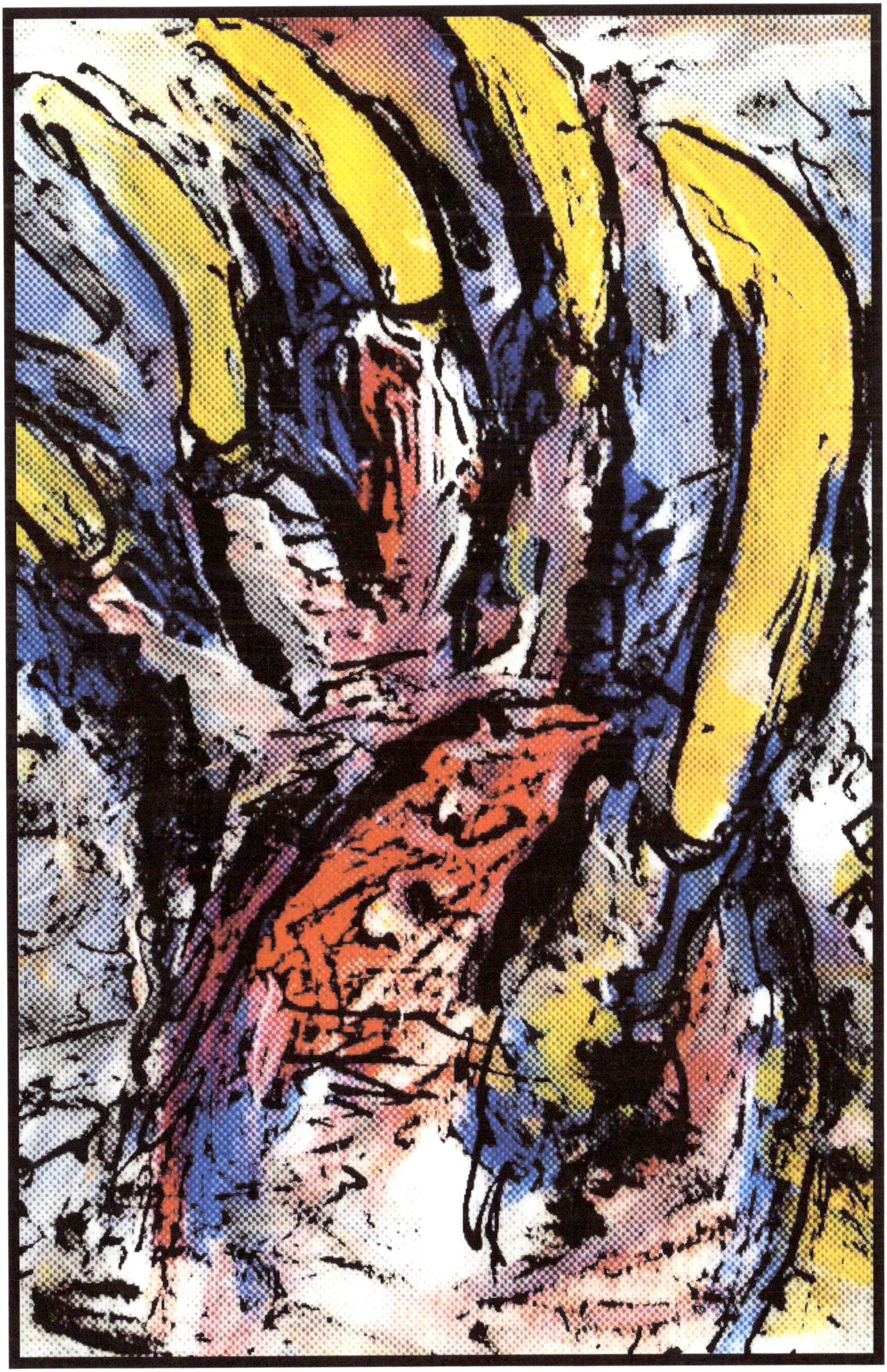

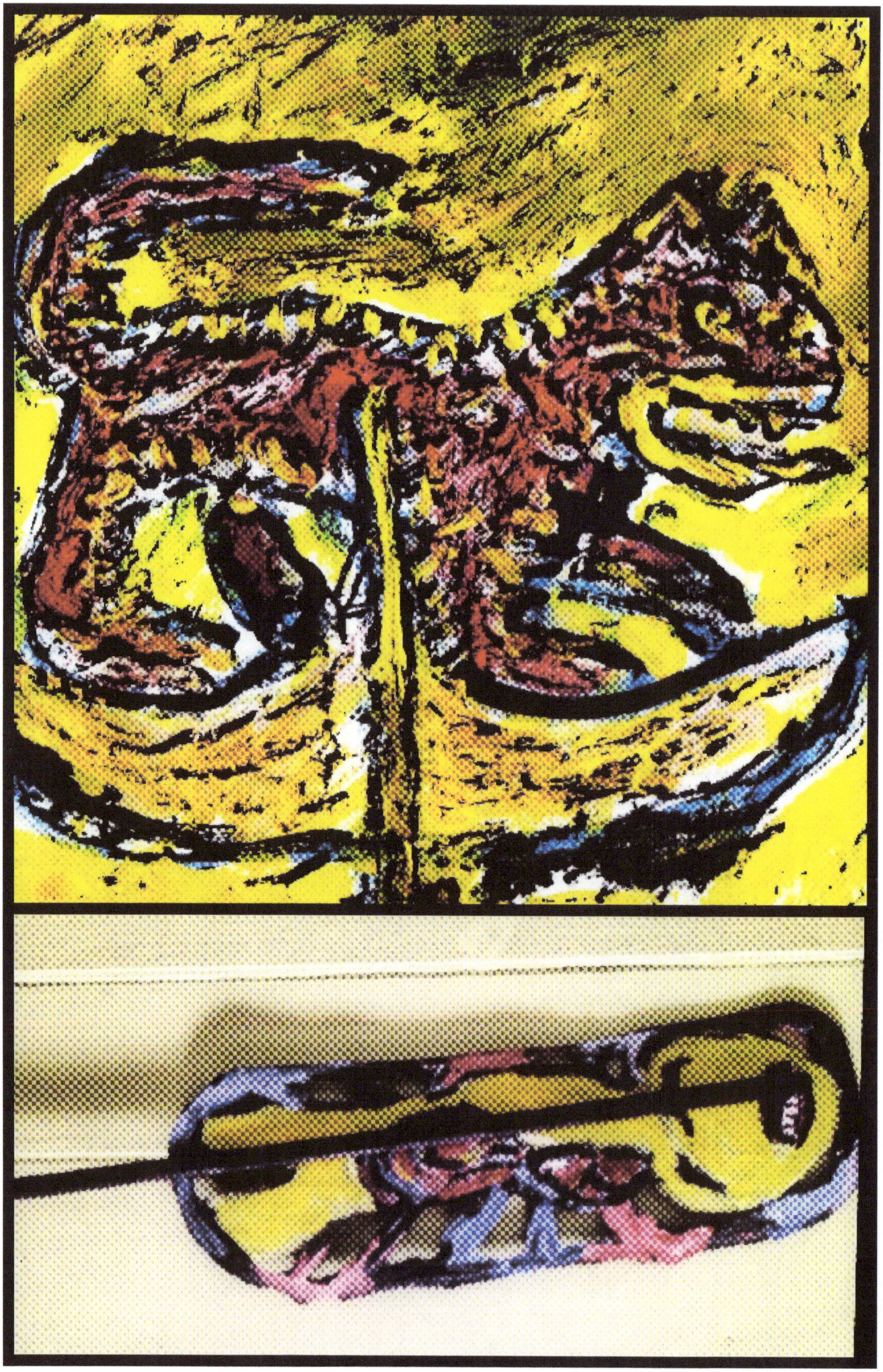

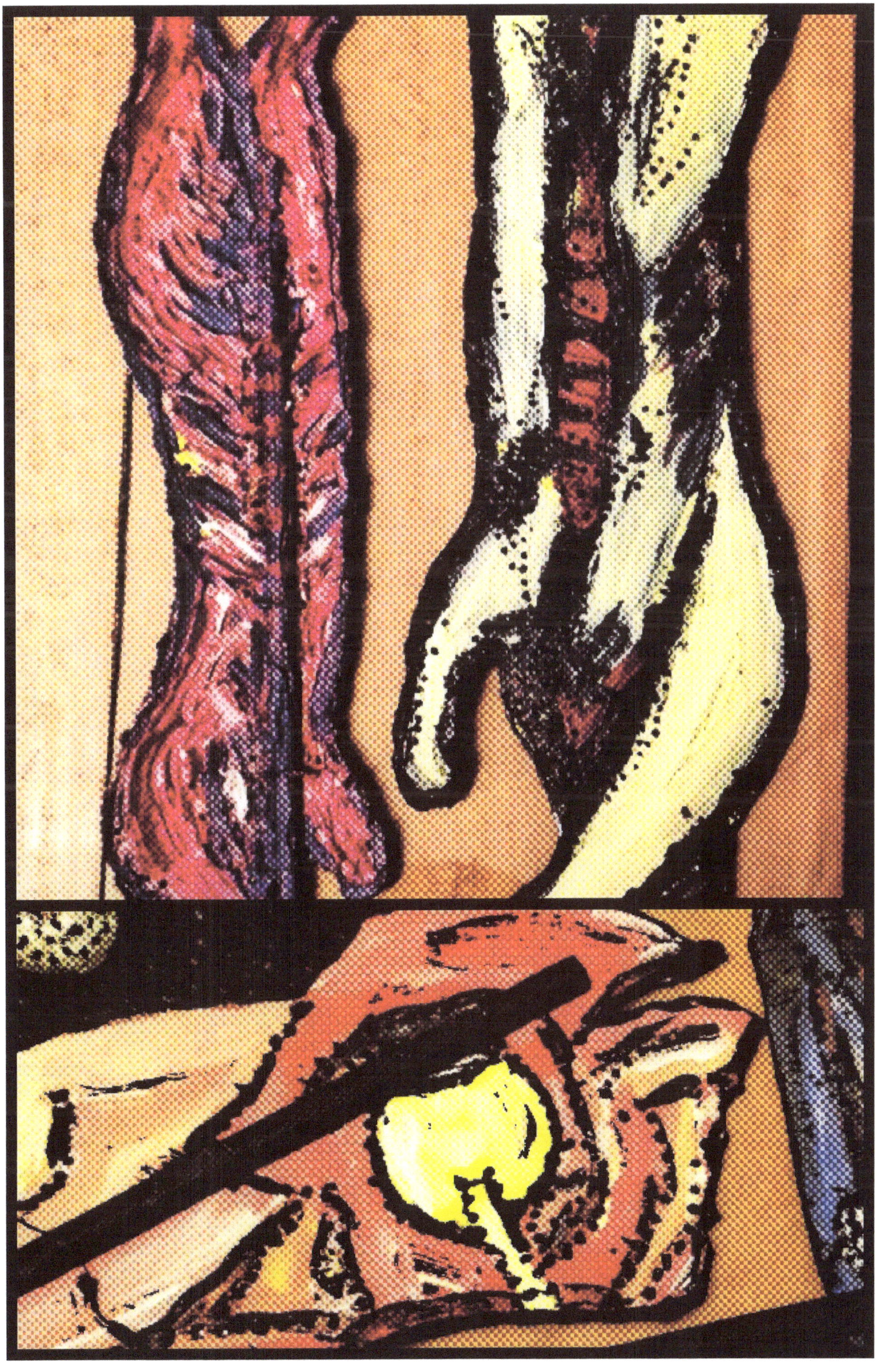

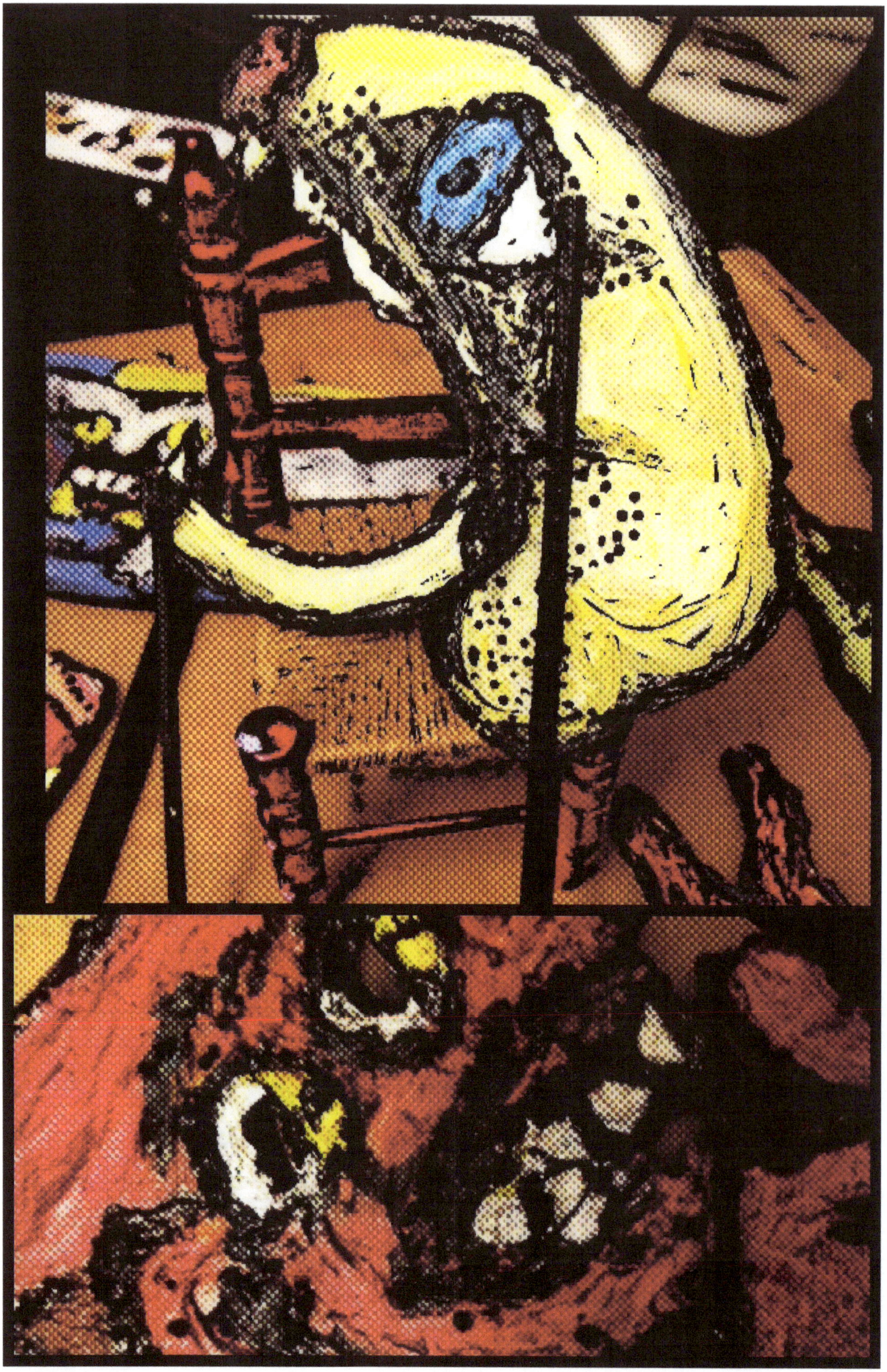

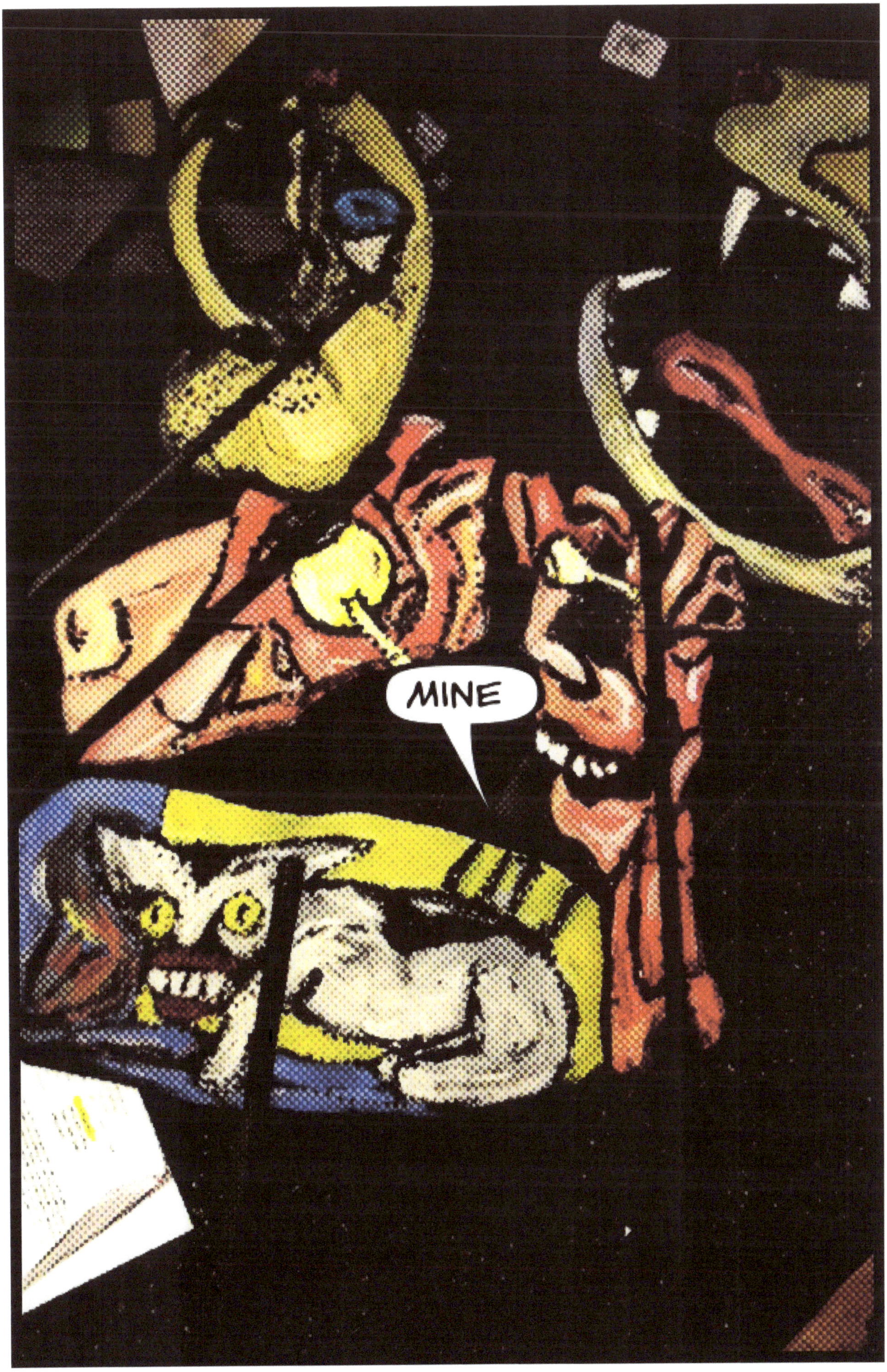
MINE

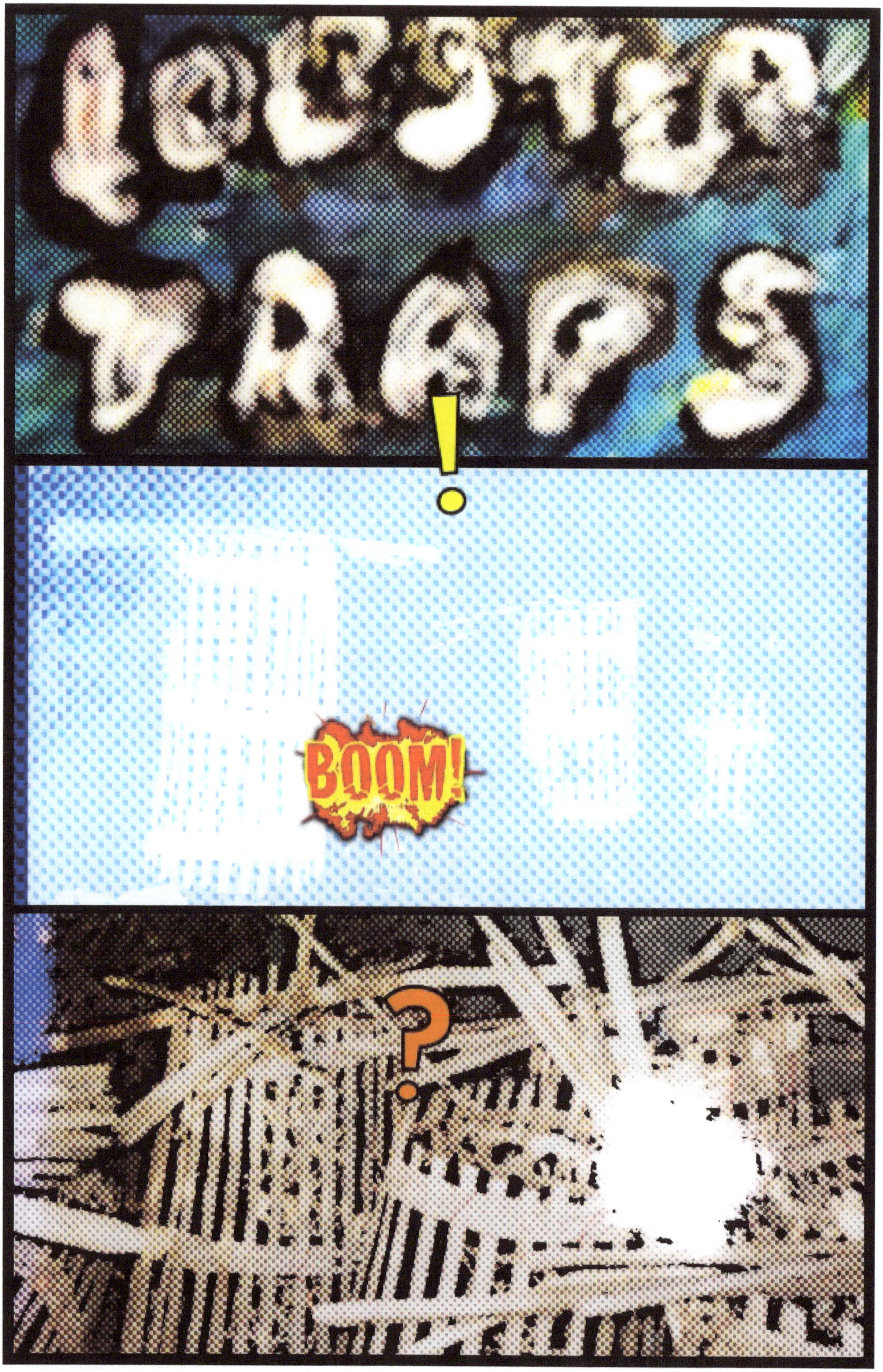
LOBSTER
TRAPS
!
BOOM!
?

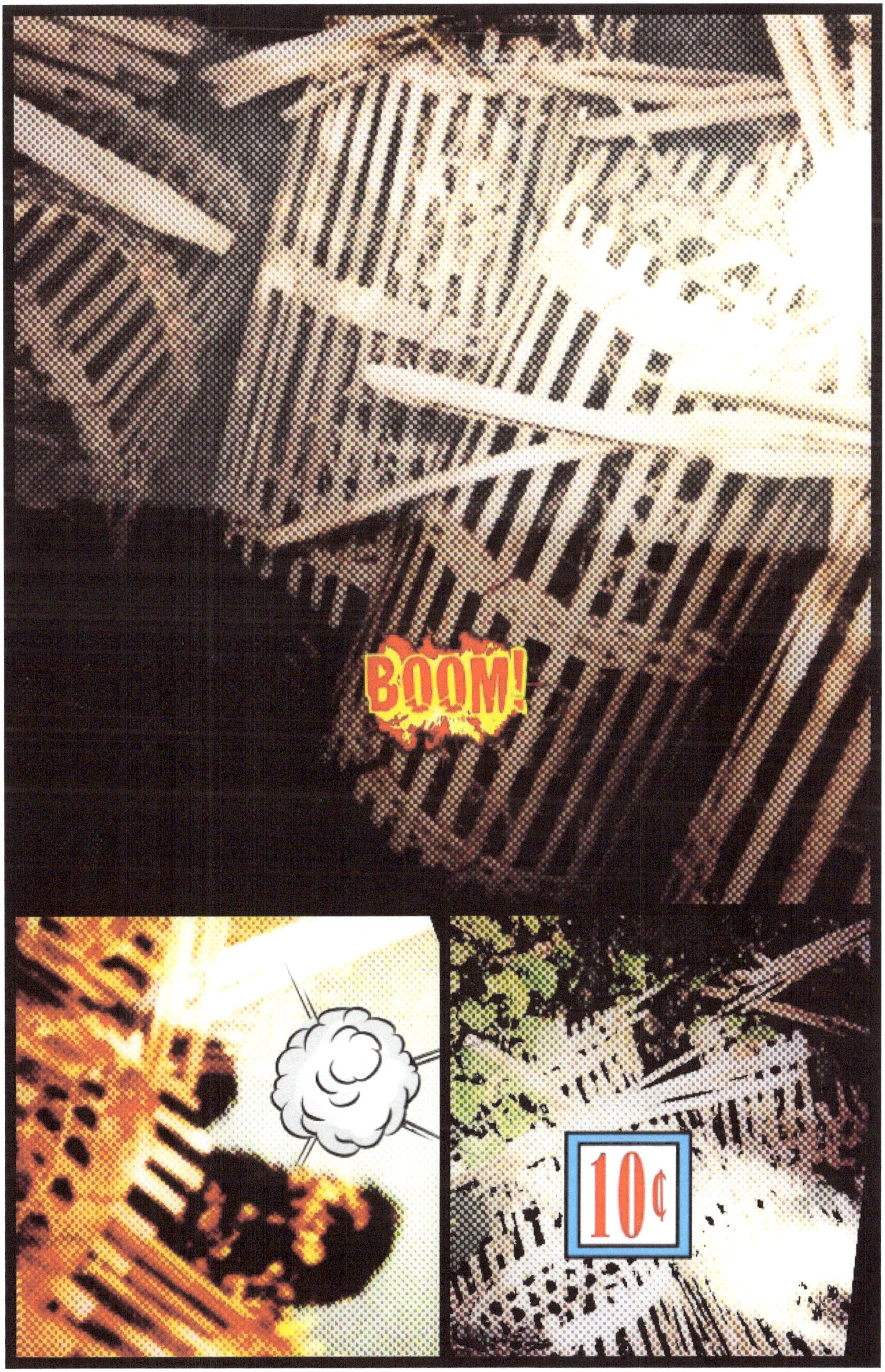
BOOM!
10¢

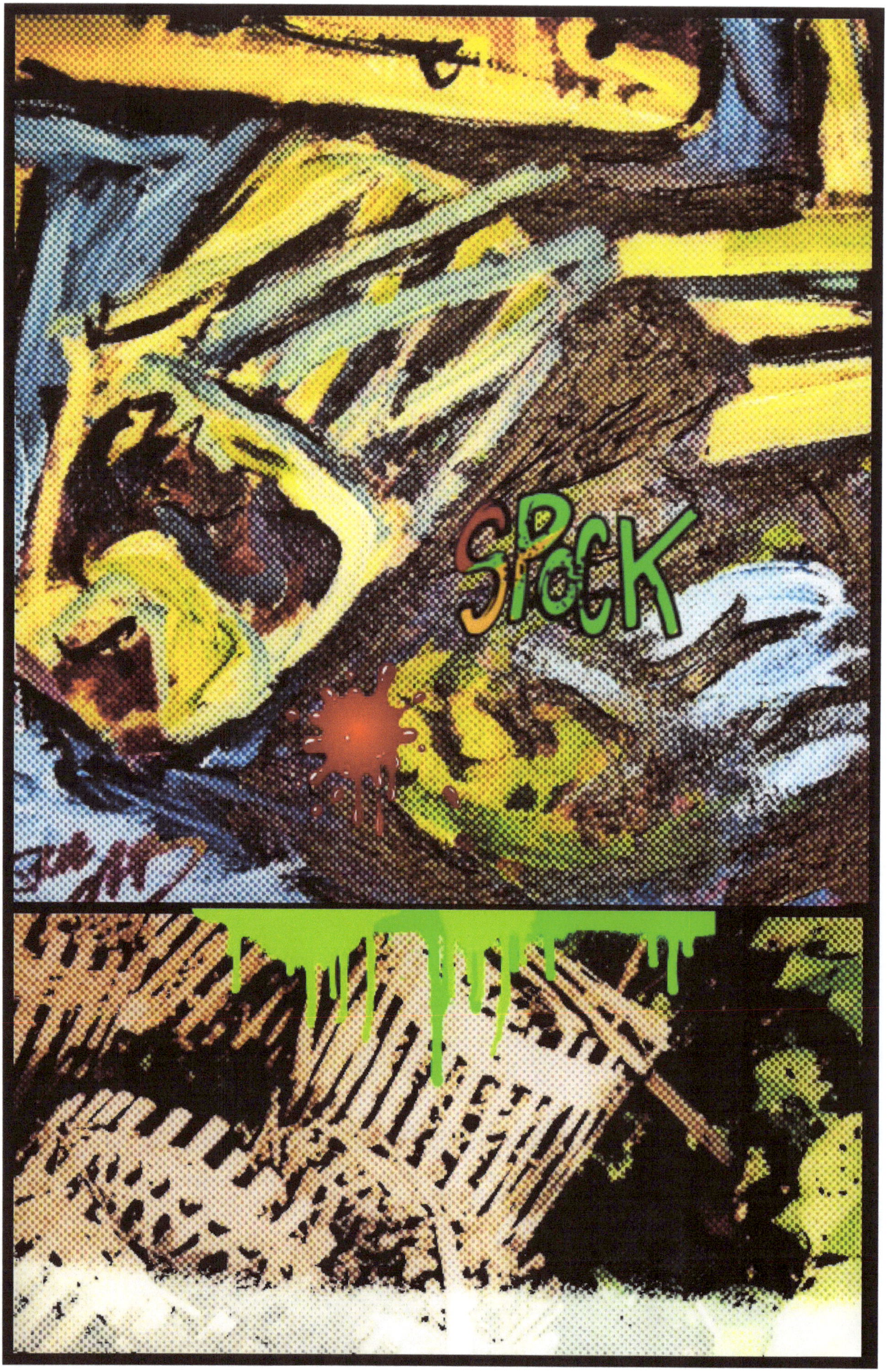
SPOCK

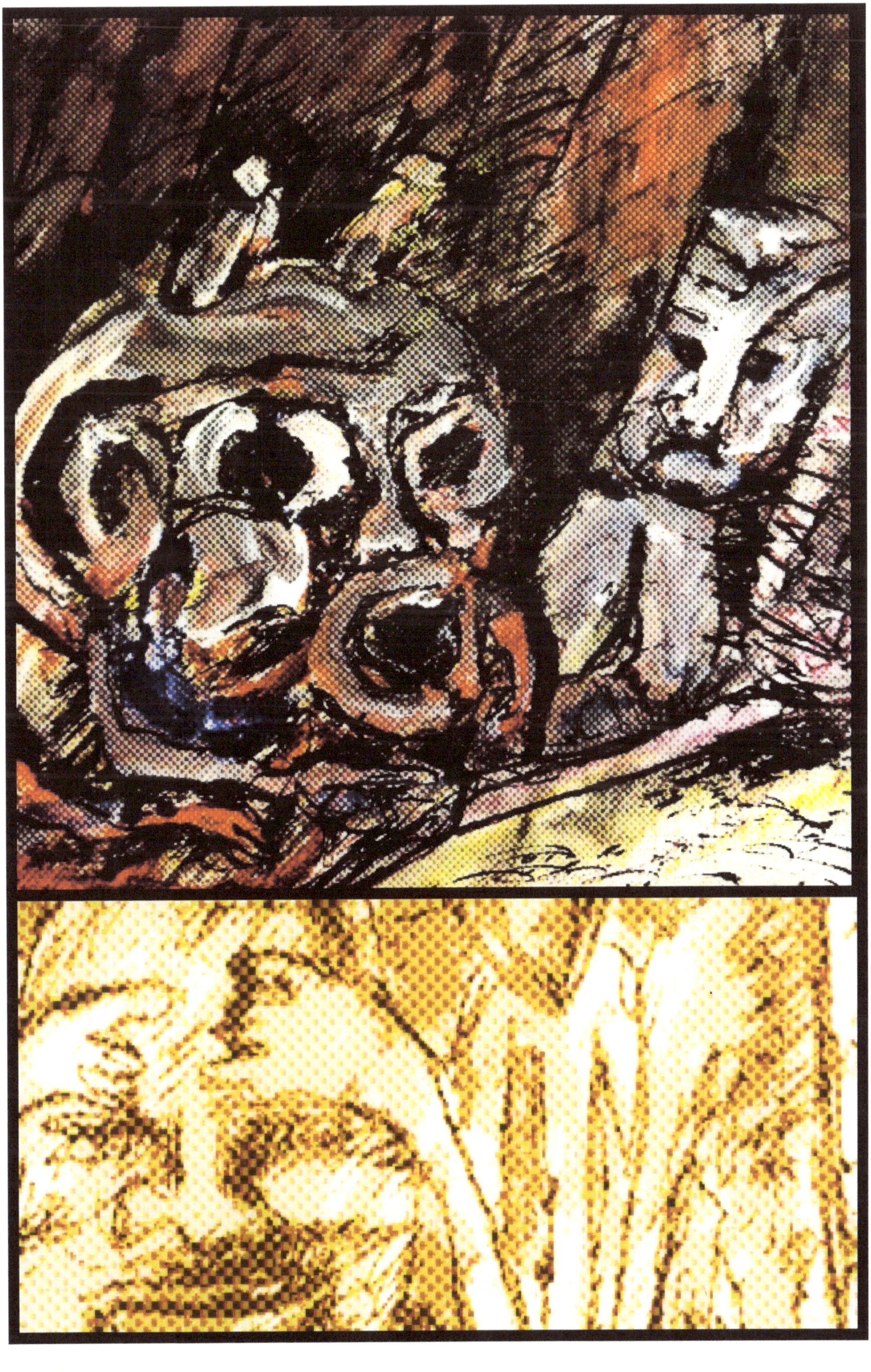

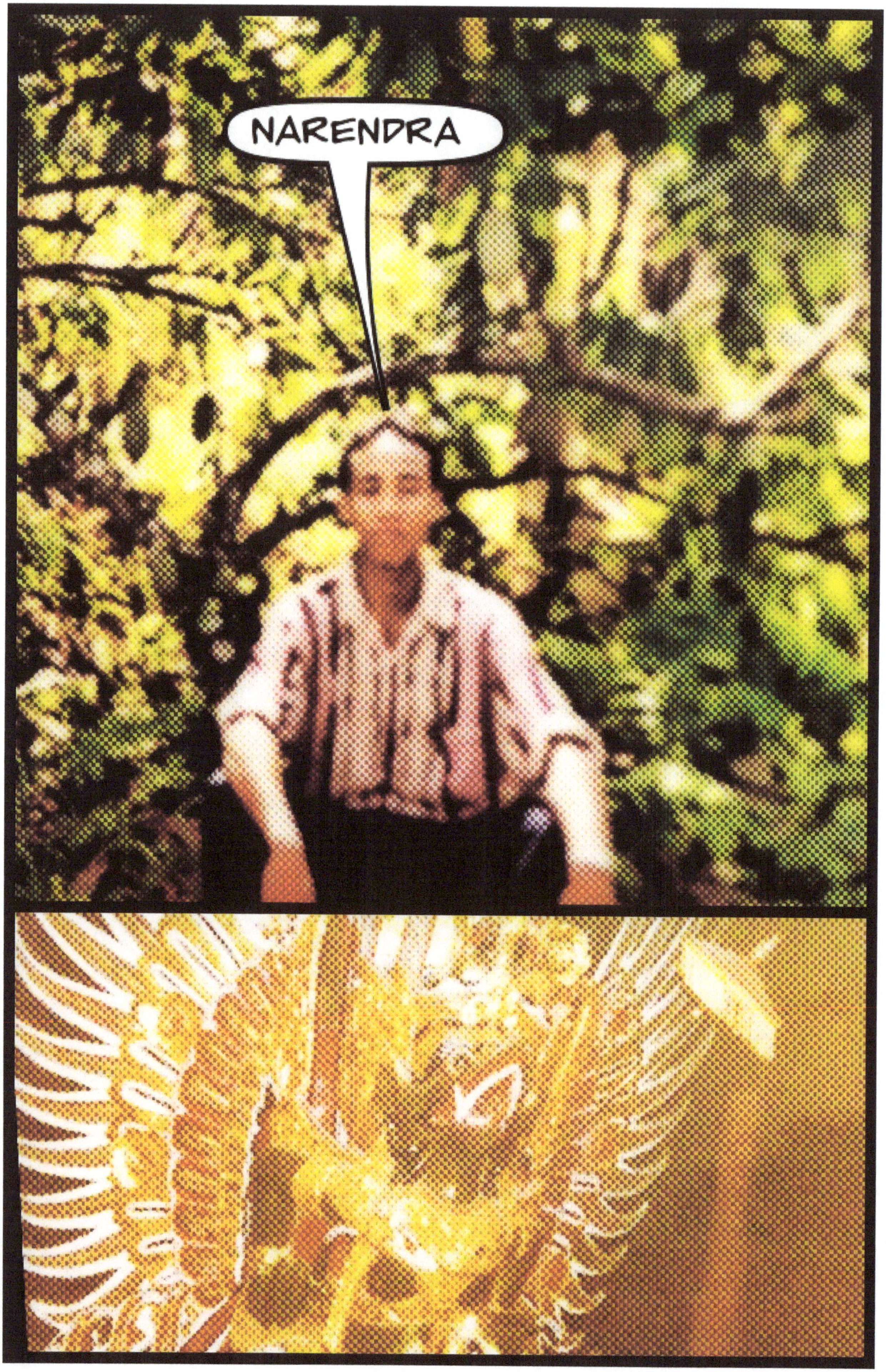
NARENDRA

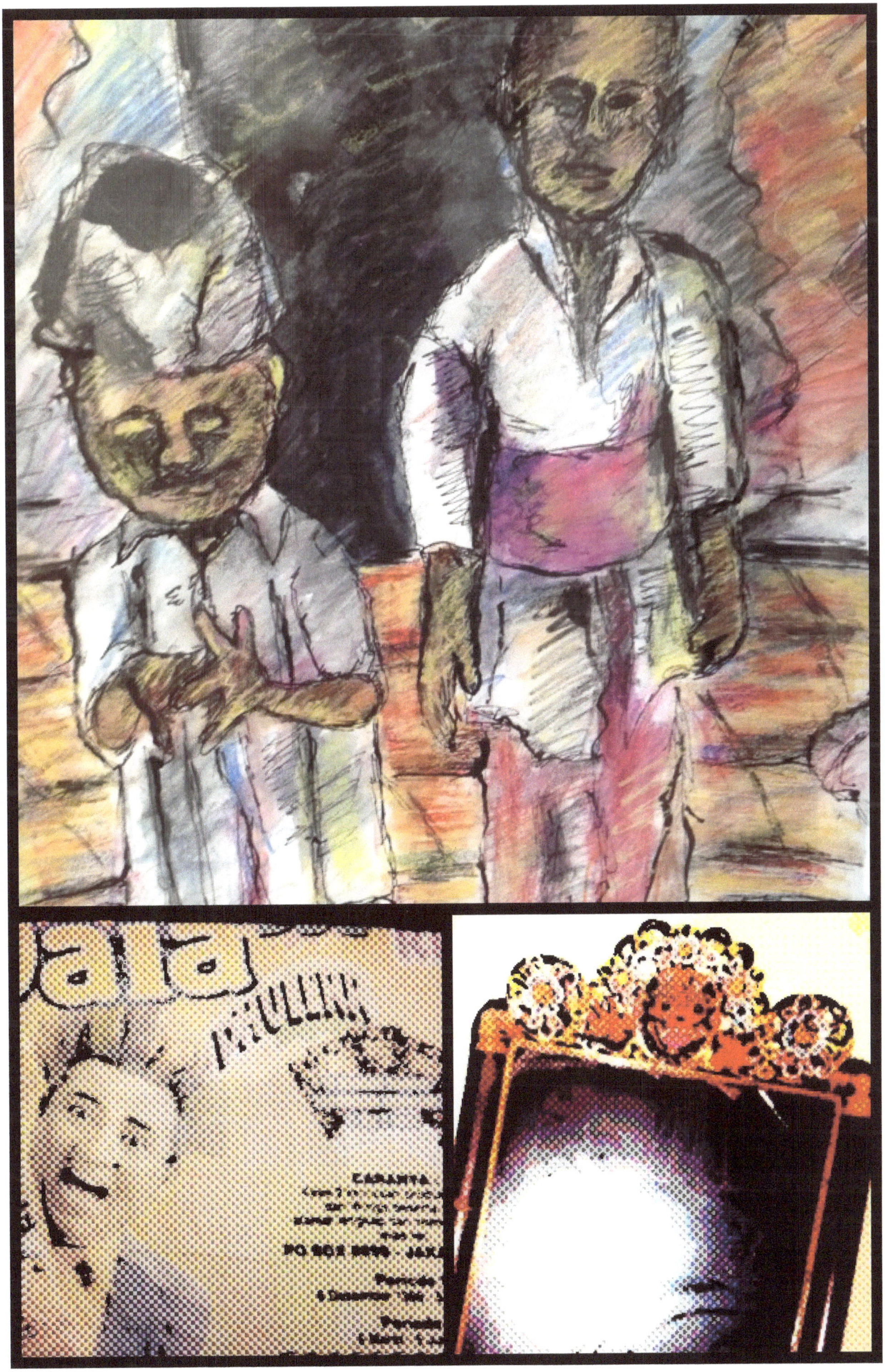

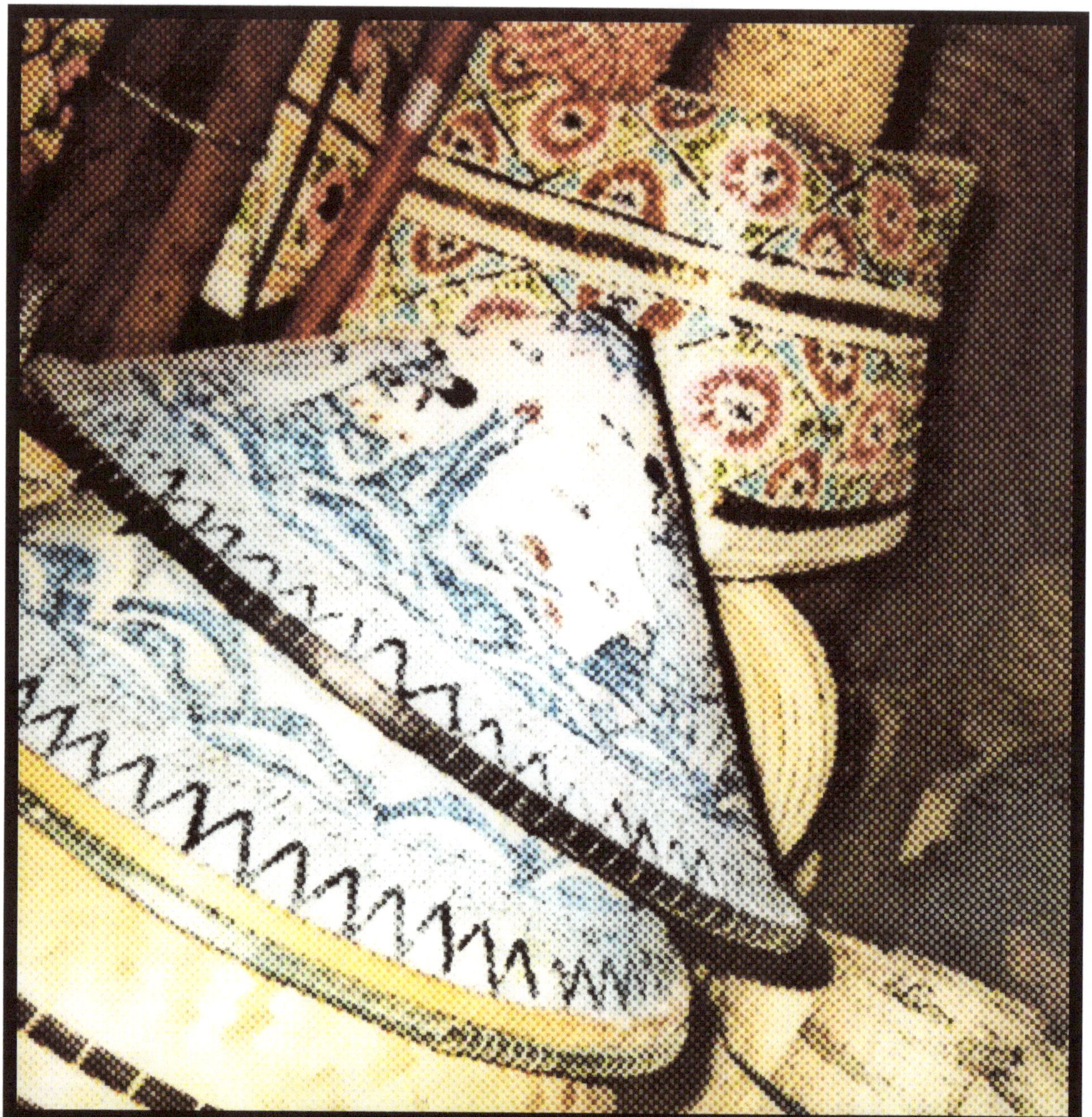

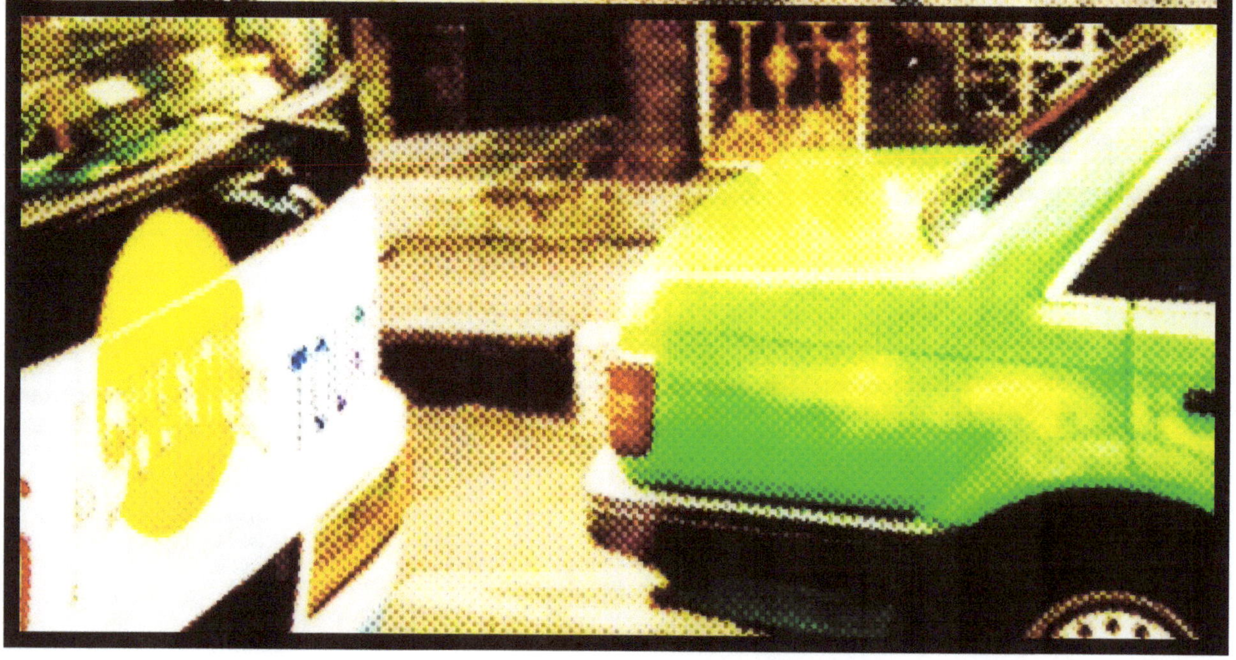

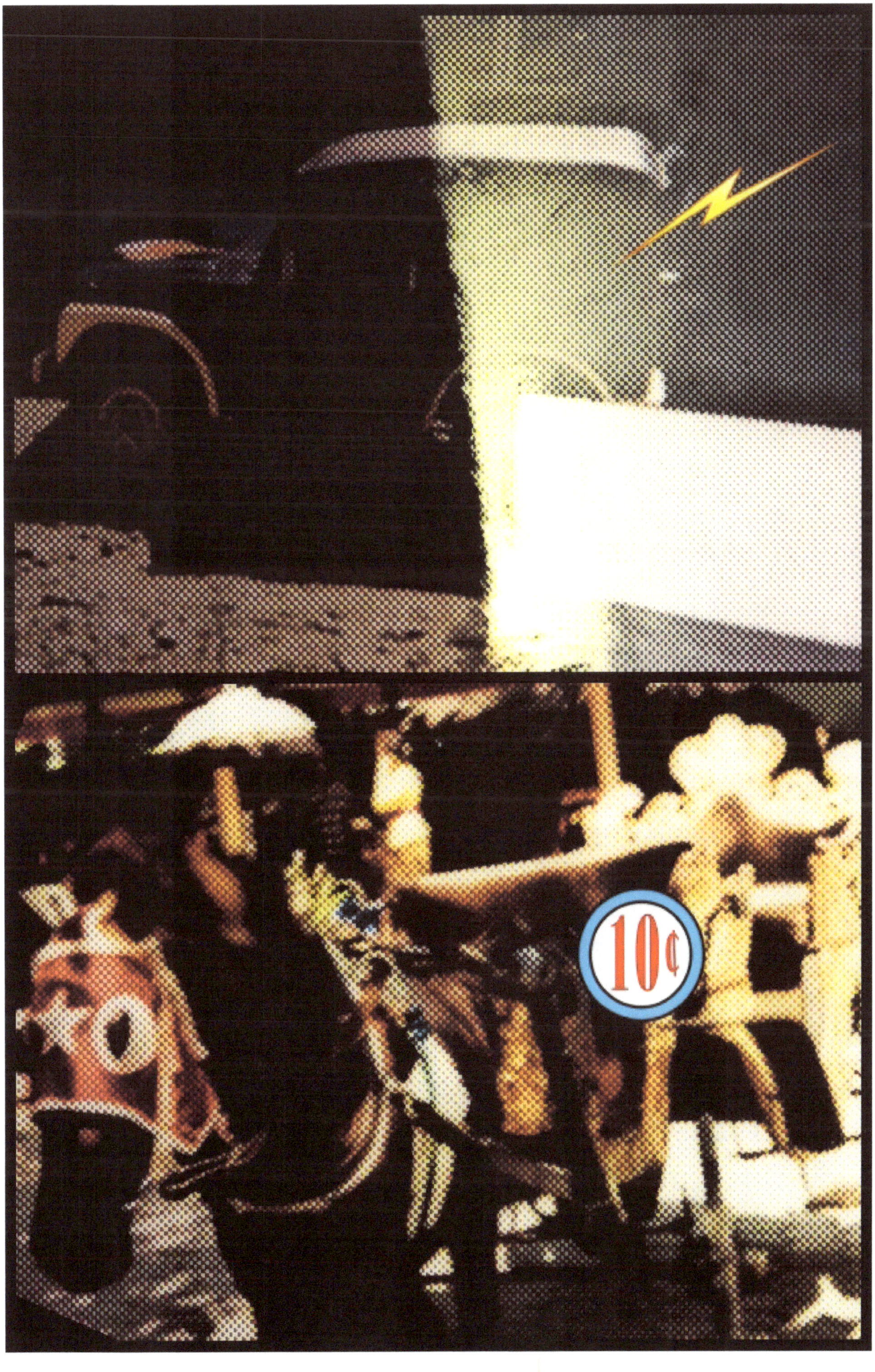
10¢

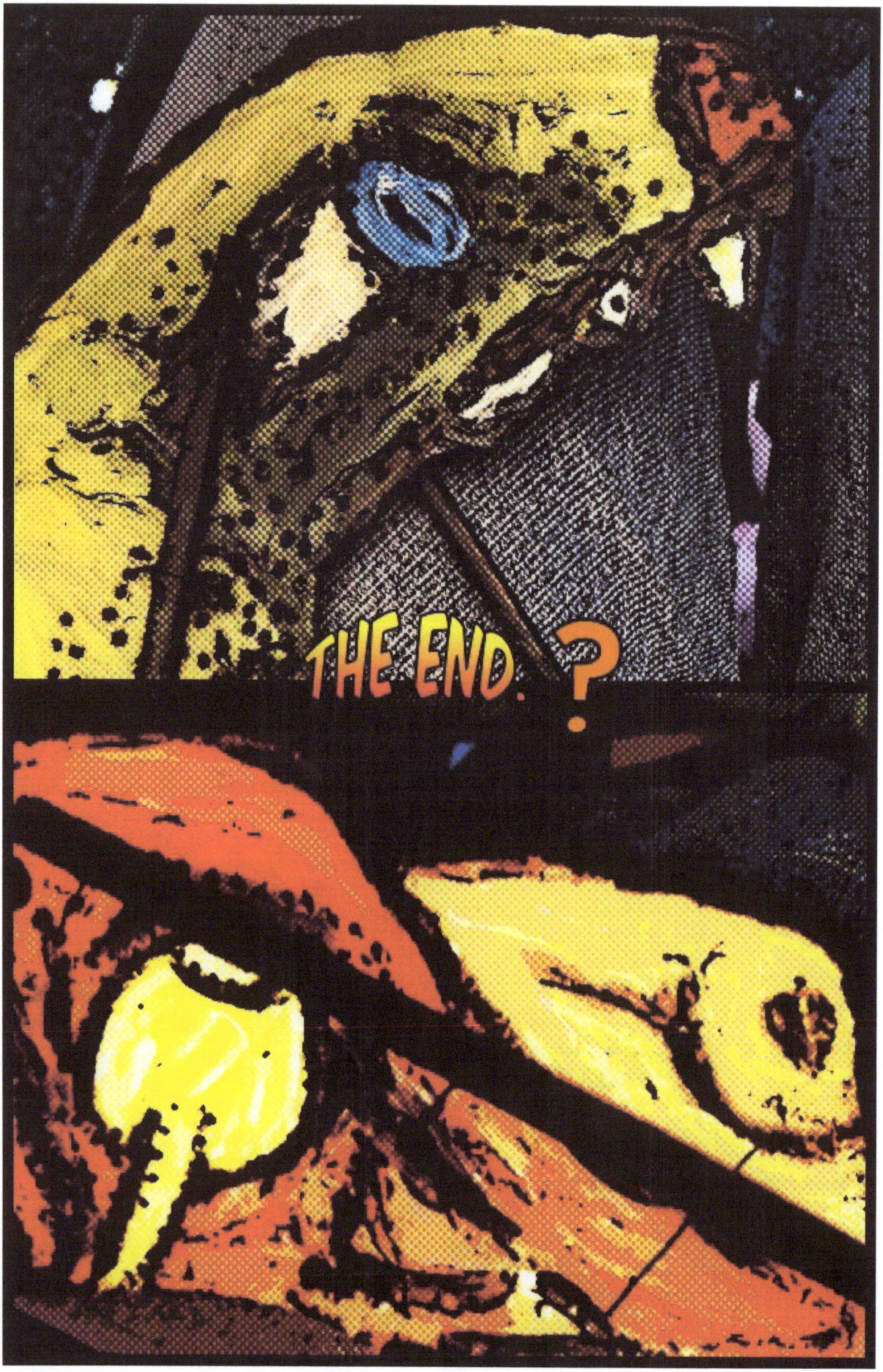
THE END. ?

www.ingramcontent.com/pod-product-compliance
Lightning Source LLC
Chambersburg PA
CBHW050903180526
45159CB00007B/2773
9781494804770